A Love That Conquers
Lauren Mitchell

ISBN-13:978-1523986866
ISBN-10:1523986867

A Love
That
Conquers

Lauren Mitchell

Contents

Forward

This book isn't about the steps you need to take to love better. It's more about the steps you can't take. Just like the Ten Commandments were never the way to create the perfect person but to show our need for God, so is Love. It's the greatest commandment, to love the Lord your God with all your heart, and with all your soul, and with all your mind and the second, to love your neighbor as yourself (Matthew 22:37-39). This comes from the mouth of Jesus. God knew that no matter how hard we try to love; we fail. That failure is meant to lead us to Him. It is meant, just like the Ten Commandments, to bring us to His feet and the end of ourselves. So this book on love is about how we can't love, and how He can. It is meant to show us the truth that with God all things are possible (Matthew 19:26).

Instructions

The format for this book incorporates a morning and an evening section for each day, five days a week. Leaving you the weekend to catch up on anything you miss. So many women have told me how much they have loved the morning and the evening that I encourage you to really try it. It works as the book ends of your day. Beginning and ending your day with God focuses the in-between time.

After each morning and evening you will incorporate these truths from scripture into your own day and your own prayer through journaling. Don't worry; there are sample prayers at the end of each day. There is additional space for you to add your own prayer at the end of both morning and evening sessions, or you can keep your prayers in your own journal. If you have never journaled a prayer in your life, pattern it after mine. I patterned mine on scripture, so you can't go wrong. Writing them will make these truths solidify in your mind. When you take a truth and add prayer you give it power.

Week 1
The end is the beginning

Week 1 Intro
The End is the Beginning

Love. We are a society that has lost this word. Not just its meaning, but the action that defines it. Satan, true to his nature, has taken this perfect thing and distorted it unrecognizably. But that isn't what this book is about. This is about a restoration to the distortion. This is about a Love that Conquers in a life where Love has seemed powerless. Love that conquers is powerful. Love, the love that God created and intended and still provides is powerful. Love is so powerful that it covers a multitude of sins. In fact it is the exact tool God used to fix the fall.

Love is patient and kind; love does not envy or boast; it is not arrogant or rude. It does not insist on its own way; it is not irritable or resentful; it does not rejoice at wrongdoing, but rejoices with the truth. Love bears all things, believes all things, hopes all things, endures all things.
1 Corinthians 13:4-7

How does reading this list make you feel? Honestly? Reading these words has made me feel powerless. It's exhausting. No seriously, just reading it makes me tired. It lists, quite frankly, things I do every day. I envy, boast, am arrogant and rude, definitely insist on my own way…like daily. And don't even get me started on irritable! When I read this, I know that I am not capable of this. However, I know that scripture says that there is no good work that God doesn't equip us for, (2 Timothy 3:17 & Hebrews 13:21). God does not expect us to
 power through this. He is totally aware of our limitations and has totally provided for them. So, what's the problem? Why aren't we able to get it together and love?

When I started researching this love list of impossible things, I found the answer. Those pairs of characteristics are distortions; at the root they are indications of something gone wrong in us. At the bottom of all the "does nots" is a misunderstanding and knowledge of God's love, or something left unhealed. All of them. What it leaves us with is cracks, places that we aren't whole. When we aren't whole, we are not a vessel that can overflow with love. God can equip us all day long, but if our vessel isn't whole, we aren't useful. It doesn't matter how hard we try we can't be conformed from the outside. We have to be transformed from the inside. Romans 12:2 shows us that we are not to be "conformed to this world, but be transformed by the renewing of your mind". We are under constant pressure to perform. That isn't what God puts on us; it's what we put on ourselves when we believe the world. We have to be transformed by renewal, not confirmed by pressure. I have determined that I will stop treating myself like Jell-O. I was not created to be pressed into a mold, but to reflect my creator.

This first week we will focus on the truth that God designed us to be filled with Himself. It's how we are supposed to bear fruit. That list in 1 Corinthians is not meant to leave us feeling powerless; it's there to point us to the Powerful. The only way that list works is to put Jesus name in the place of Love. Jesus is patient and kind; Jesus does not envy or boast; Jesus is not arrogant or rude. Jesus does not insist on His own way; Jesus is not irritable or resentful; Jesus does not rejoice at
wrongdoing but rejoices with the truth. Jesus bears all things, believes all things, hopes all things, and endures all things. Abiding in Jesus invites Him to abide in us, and then all things are possible.

I need you to know that in that all the things that we are going to study are not things I have mastered. I haven't learned to love better yet. That isn't really what this is about. This is about realizing that in my failure to love, I am loved. God knew when he inspired this description of love to be penned that we could never attain it. We weren't meant to. It was meant to get us to the end of ourselves. For me, that has worked. I can say that at this point in my life I can get to the end of myself pretty quickly. That is what has led me to figure love out. Because knowing that we could never love perfectly on our own, God still made it the greatest commandment. We are missing the secret. That is what I want us to find.

Day 1   *Read John 15:1-17*

Love, it's the hardest command that masquerades as something that should come naturally. Why is loving people so hard? The problem with love is not people; it's sin. Read that last sentence again and let it sink in. Loving is hard because of sin. I am not battling people; I am battling either their sin or my sin. When I am frustrated to tears with my husband or children, it's really about sin not about who they are. Sin makes it hard to love, not the people. Sin wrecks love! It's what wrecked love in the beginning. What did God send to fix it? He sent Love. The tool that the all powerful God used to fix sin; Love. Love is the tool Jesus used to redeem us. That is what held him to that cross. That is how he conquered sin, and it's how we conquer sin too. Love is what conquers sin, because Jesus is love! When I am not enough; He is.

God is Love. Love is Jesus. They are synonymous. You cannot love without Jesus. Jesus himself is Love. Saying that Love is not irritable or resentful, doesn't make me not irritable or resentful. Memorizing the verses doesn't make me patient and kind. There is no power in the words, they don't change me; He changes me. The only way I can love is Jesus. It's so simple that it's amazing to me how much I miss it. It's the gospel. Christ in me.

I can't rely on my own feelings for love. Feelings are far too fickle and fragile things to depend on for power or motivation, yet that's what I do all the time. When I fail loved ones I often lament: but I love them so much! My love isn't enough; it will fail, but His love is always enough.

I am not telling you that Love is a verb and we need a plan and we need to try harder. Most of the time, I can't try harder! <u>I am here to tell you I need Jesus. I've hit the end of me. Love is not something I can conjure up, it's a person's identity that I need to put on. Faith in God's love for us, relying on God's love for us, and being empowered by abiding in God's love for us is the only hope we have of loving.</u>

Verse 11 clearly tells us that abiding in God is the way for his joy to be in us and our joy to be full. At the conclusion of the passage we read this morning it tells us that these things He has commanded us, so that we will love one another. The thing he commanded us to do was to abide in His love. God doesn't say, "Go, bear fruit!" he says abide in me and fruit will come.

Father, help me see that I have hit the end of myself and that all my striving needs to cease. You know the depravity in me, and you also know the power living in me. Help me to see it too and to access it as you intended so that I can live a life of love that my love will prove your love to those watching (John 13:35). God, we need a love that we are lacking, you are It. We pray simply for more of you.
Your turn

Copy the verses here, but every time the word "love" is used you write "Jesus".

Day 2   *Read 1 John 4:7-19*

"So we have come to know and to believe the love that God has for us. God is love, and whoever abides in love abides in God, and God abides in him."1 John 4:16 ESV

Go back to that verse and underline the two things that we are to do with the love God has for us.

Before we can abide in love we have to *know* and *believe* the love God has for us. I love how the NIV phrases this "we *know* and *rely* on the love God has for us". The NIV replaces "believe" with "rely".

The first sentence of 1 John 4:16 is pivotal! It took me forever to see the extent of the meaning. It implies that we are to know and believe the love that God loves us with, the depth of His feelings for us. But I saw another meaning also. It also implies that we are to *know* and *believe* or rely on the love that God has for us; meaning that love is available to us, or love that He puts at our disposal. Not only does our being able to love depend on *knowing* and *believing* that God loves us, but He puts that same love at our disposal and we can rely on Him for the power and strength to love. The way to tap in to that power and rely on it is explained in the second sentence of this same verse; "God is love and whoever abides in love abides in God and God abides in him." Abiding in God is how we love. I know…it's that simple! We can close the book and finish the study, right? Unfortunately, we have to dredge out the practical and usually complicated way this actually works out in real life.

To be capable of love you have to abide in Love. We have to let go of expectations that we put on ourselves and understand that we cannot do this, then rely on the love God has for us. Not just that He loves us, but the Love He puts at our disposal.

God, open my eyes to see what I am not capable of and let that realization propel me to your feet. Help me to know and believe not just that you love me, but that because of your love you have put Jesus at my disposal. You have set him in my heart! He is everything needed for life and godliness. He is everything needed for love. Teach me to abide and out of that abiding let love flow. Your turn...

There is no fear in love. This one sentence tells so much of my life. I have so often abided in fear instead of Love. The reason: I have not been perfected in Love. I haven't understood God's love for me really, only in part. For a lot of my life I have chosen obedience out of fear of punishment. Understanding God's love enables us to choose obedience out of love. The reason it is so hard is because the temporal world we live in obeys out of fear, even often in the Christian realm. We are a people group who has not understood the relationship that is Christianity. We haven't really grasped all that God has offered us; all that He wants to give us.

Sin ushered fear into our world. When God fixed the problem of sin with Love (Jesus), He fixed the problem of fear. Perfect Love casts out fear. But Satan still gets us to play his games of fear and guilt. When we fail, God wants us to turn to Him not away from Him in fear like the Israelites. If we don't understand His constant love, then we turn away in shame and hide, just like Adam and Eve did in the garden. Running to Him in our failure changes everything; it gives Him access to our hearts where He can make His love known.

"God sees something redemptive even in letting us fail. He seems less concerned about our mistakes than how we respond to them." Wayne Jacobsen

God, show me how to be perfected in Love and cast out my fear of punishment. Help me understand and operate more out of the love you have for me.

Transfer it from head knowledge to heart function.
Show me how to love because you first loved me.
It's the only way love works.
Your turn

"...if we love one another, God abides in us and his love is *perfected* in us." (v12b)

"God is love, and whoever abides in love abides in God, and God abides in him. By this is love *perfected* with us..." (v16b&17a)

Love is only perfected when time is spent with the Perfect. Verses 12 &17 practically shout this at us. The reason we are on earth and not immediately taken to heaven is perfection. We are here to be made fit for heaven. That perfecting takes time. There is no way around it and no shortcut. Love is not legalistic, but it does take discipline. Let's face it, discipline does not happen when you do something twice a week. Abiding in God is a discipline just like any other, and it takes continued focus. If you want victory in the everyday, then you have to abide with God in the everyday. You have to practice in every day, every hour, and every minute. It takes training and time. There is no short cut.

Love is a battle and lots of it takes place in the trenches of the mundane things. If you aren't abiding and walking with God, you aren't ready for battle. Navy seals don't go into battle without training and time and focus. We aren't supposed to either. We have to train ourselves to see the truth and focus on God's presence with us. We can't spend little time on training and expect to be prepared to battle sin and love people. It just doesn't logically follow that that would work. In the heat of the battle to love, calling on God won't work if you aren't familiar with Him enough to hear His answer. There is a time and place for arrow prayers, but they are not effective if we haven't honed our senses in to hit the target.

We treat time with Jesus as something that enhances our spiritual life when in actuality it is the only thing that enables our spiritual life. Without Jesus, there is no love. Without love, we are nothing. According to 1 Corinthians 13 we are no more than, "a resounding gong or clanging cymbal". Galatians 5:6 b says, "The only thing that counts is faith expressing itself through love." I want my time here to count!!! I don't want to just keep doing the same thing and failing. I want to be being perfected and sanctified. Learning to love is an everyday process that Jesus is using to perfect us.

If you want to your husband...family...friends...church, it's the only way. Jesus has to do the work in me. Abiding in Him gives the access to my heart where He can work.

Father, I want my time to count. I understand that love is a tool to perfect me. Help me to embrace it. Show me where I am lacking love and speak your love over me so that I don't feel guilt but only conviction. Help me choose to be perfected by choosing time with the Perfect. Train me for battle. Strengthen my heart, I don't want to be fainthearted, but of good courage!
Your Turn

How do we become more rooted and grounded in love?

Father, we pray that Christ dwelling in our hearts strengthens our faith and grows deeper roots of Love into our hearts. Let it so entwine every part of us that we become grounded in your love which becomes our motivation for obedience and our soft place to fall when we fail.
Your turn

Day 4   Read 1 Corinthians 13:8-13

"Reality is a leading cause of stress among those in touch with it."

This quote made me laugh till I almost cried from the truth of it! Reality, isn't that totally the problem! If I could just check out of reality for like 24 hours, I could rid myself of a lot of stress! The day in and day out of reality and time marching forward is enough to cause us all to lament with Solomon in Ecclesiastes 1 "Meaningless, Meaningless! Everything is meaningless" (NIV). The problem isn't reality. The problem is we are confused about our identity. We don't end when this life is over. Our life only begins when this life is over. We aren't temporal but eternal. Our identity makes us joint heirs with Christ" (Romans 8:17), that is our *true* reality. We can't see it, so we don't act as if it's the truth. That is why contact with God everyday is so important. What we can see will be more real to us than what is actually real unless we train ourselves to see more of God. He is the most real unseen. We have to look with eyes like Moses and train ourselves to see Him, (Hebrews 11:27). Repeated contact with God throughout the day refocuses us on the Truth. It trains our eyes to see more clearly what is real. Each time we reach for God and reaffirm the truth it's like breathing. It's fresh air that makes everything different. God's presence changes my reality. Abiding in God's love doesn't involve hours of time, it can, but it's mostly about a faithful reaching for Him first thing followed by a day of Him in the moments. It's not about fitting Him into your moments; it's about turning all your moments to Him, making them about Him. Everything we make about Him turns into Love. Cleaning toilets, dirty diapers, screaming children, sleepless nights, dirty dishes, everything meaningless gets meaning! If we reach for God in our need, it glorifies Him because it changes our focus from our need to His abundant supply. Real love shows God's glory, not ours because it is evident that He abides in us when we accomplish what *we* could not. "And this is his commandment that we believe in the name of his Son Jesus Christ and love one another, just as he has commanded us. Whoever keeps his commandments abides in God and God in him. And by this we know that he abides in us, by the Spirit whom he has given us", (1 John 3:23&24).

In our reading this morning, Paul talked about the fact that when the Perfect comes the partial will pass away. We know that Perfect is Jesus, all the rest is going to pass away. And for now we see only dimly in a mirror, but the more we focus on that Perfect, the more we see. Then, when the Perfect comes, we will know fully even as we have been fully known. Being *fully known* is being fully loved. And then Paul leaves us with what lasts, when the partial passes away the only thing that will be left: "Faith, Hope, and Love. And the greatest of these is Love". Everything done for Love will turn right into Jesus and He is our prize! When I would read verse 13 I used to always wonder, why is the greatest of these love? The greatest is Love because Love is Jesus.

We read in Galatians yesterday that Faith expressing itself through love is all that counts! It's a love that springs from your belief that God loves you. You want to make those dirty diapers count? Sing to God while you are changing them. When it gets hard instead of focusing on now, refocus on **Reality** and realize that it's an opportunity for love to count. Reach for Love and realize that you are already fully known and fully loved. The more you practice the more you will see clearly. Just say Jesus name and He will show up. I am not saying this is easy. I am just starting to work this out in my life and I will be working on it till the Perfect comes or I go home, but I am determined that *it*, no matter what the *it* in my day may be, is going to count for Love!

What is the *It* in your day that you need to turn into Jesus?

Meet me in the morning and help me to choose this time with you because it is all that holds me fast to what is real. Teach me how to really breathe. Help me refocus over and over as many times as it takes until I see my Reality more clearly.
Your turn

Refocusing on God when we have not met our expectations is a habit we need to start practicing. We need to maintain the focus of God's love for us so that we maintain hope in the midst of failure. God wants us to turn to Him not into ourselves. When we turn to Him, our inability is swallowed up by His ability to do far more than all we ask or imagine (Ephesians 3:20). When Love can live in and through us, God is glorified. It is evidence of His spirit in us and it is more than that, love is the language God speaks to our hearts. When you are enabled to love the Holy Spirit can speak perfectly through you to reach the one you are seeking to love.

What are some practical ways we can refocus on God throughout the day?

Why are we so tempted to turn away from God when we fail?

God, help me turn to you automatically when I fall short. Change my reaction of despair at my failure to a declaration of your ability. Instead of wallowing in my need, open my eyes to see that you wait to fill me. All I need do is ask. As I seek you in my day, help be to better perceive your presence.

Your turn

Verse 14's key words, "controls us"! Not sin, not the situation ...us. That is how we win. Satan doesn't see it coming. He sees us trying to fight against the people or the circumstance itself. It doesn't make sense that Love conquers sin; it is gentle and kind. Logically it doesn't follow that love would be strong enough to combat something so ugly. It's like the secret weapon that we can't understand until we obey and wield it.

<u>The more you let Christ fully love you the more you feel safety in His control.</u> We don't live for ourselves, because He lives for us. We don't have to look out for ourselves because He does. I don't have to manipulate people to fill my needs because He fills my needs. We have to let the love of Christ control us, not our reactions, perceived needs, grievances, guilt, or desires for our own glory. That is when Love really conquers. We are going to get into the nitty gritty and step all over some toes! There is sin in us, and it wrecks our ability to love. But the good news is in Proverbs 10:12, "Hatred stirs up strife, but love covers all offenses". This is the good news!!! Jesus is love! He covers us! Sin may wreck love because the sin in us distorts our love, but we no longer have to be us. Ephesians 4:22-24 tells us to put off our old self and to put on the new self. When we put on Christ, He covers all our offenses. When we put Him on we are capable of things only He can do.

There is no better way to say this than how Steven Curtis Chapman does;
"Love, take these words that I'm speaking,
Love, take these thoughts that I'm thinking.
Love, take me over.
Love, fill up all of my space and

Love stand right here in my place."

I heard you, you sang it didn't you. Go back and read the words. Notice that Love is capitalized because it is referring to a person. I need Love to fill up all of my space and stand right here in my place. I need Love to take me over!

God let the responsibility of love weigh heavily enough on me that I give you control. Let me not even contemplate being enough on my own. I confess and know that I am not. Let me abide so closely with you that I can love those you give me. Cover me; show me how to put you on in every moment and every situation. Help me fight for love when I am tired. Help me remember it isn't the people who make me tired, it's the sin.
Your turn

"For God is working in you,
giving you the desire and the power to do what pleases him."
Philippians 2:13

What is an area that you feel you lack either the desire or the power to please God?

Father, as we prepare for this next week, give us the courage we need to let you work in us. Thank you that you give us not only the power to do what you ask, but the desire when it is lacking. Give us the desire to learn to love others for your glory. Give us the desire to grow and then provide the power we need.

Your turn

Week 2
Love does not envy or boast

Week 2 Intro
Love does not envy or boast

When I started really studying that list of things in 1 Corinthians 13, I found that at the root of all of them is something gone wrong. The collection of things that Love does not do is given to us in pairs. I figured God had a reason and started noticing that the words paired together were related to a distinct root. There were two main root problems that I found. At the bottom of all the "does nots" is either a hurt or pain that has created fissures in our souls that we have not allowed God to fully heal, or a sin that leaves us with a gaping hole we haven't let God fully deal with. All of them fit in one of those two categories.

According to John 15 verse 11, abiding in God makes us full. The problem with loving people isn't that God doesn't give us what we need to love; it's that we aren't equipped to hold it. In 1 Thessalonians 3:12, Paul prays that the Lord would make their love increase and overflow for each other. We can't overflow with love for people because we have cracks; we're leaking. Our cracks come in one of two main root problems. You guessed it, our cracks are either things we haven't let God fully heal or sins we haven't let Him fully deal with. Before we can abound in love for each other, we have to let God deal with our cracks. Our problem is that we just keep trying to fill the cup, and God always provides, but then before it can overflow it seeps right out those cracks. We can't hold the abundance until we're whole. The good news is that God is in the business of taking vessels and making them whole and fit for use.

The next weeks of this study deal with those pairs of words from Corinthians and the root that links them together. This next week's words come from "love does not envy or boast". The words envy and boast are related to the lie we often believe; we are not enough. Satan feeds it to us all the time, everywhere we look. Just like his other deceptions, when we believe it, it leads to sin. To really love, we have to let God deal with this sin in us.

Envy can kill a relationship and make it incredibly painful instead of beneficial as God intended. We cannot love until we put down the weapon of comparison. Satan uses it to destroy the one who wields it. It slowly eats away at the heart like gangrene and consumes all thankfulness and joy.

Boasting happens when we feel the emptiness of our cup and believe the lies that not only are we not enough, but God has not given enough. We seek to fill our cup ourselves. Ironically it leaves us even emptier. Lies always do.

Before there can be unity in the body of Christ or any building up in love we have to put away this lie. God can shine light on the places we have believed it and that Light will dispel all the darkness. God will replace this lie we have believed with the truth that every good and perfect gift comes from the father of lights who never changes (James 1:17).

Day 1   **Read 1 Timothy 1:5** *(in a couple translations if possible)*

"The purpose of my instruction is that all believers would be filled with love that comes from a pure heart, a clear conscience, and genuine faith."

1 Timothy 1:5 (NLT)

Paul indicates that being filled with love starts with a pure heart. I think that a clear conscience and genuine faith are quick to follow a pure heart. The one in turn produces the others. When we don't have a pure heart, it leads to hiding or desperately trying to cover. What is it that made Adam and Eve hide in the garden? According to Genesis 3:8, it was the presence of God. They knew that in His presence their motives and hearts would be totally transparent. The Light can't help but expose darkness. They reacted in fear, but we aren't like Adam and Eve. Our sin has already been paid for allowing us freedom from guilt and shame. Remember 1John 4:18, "there is no fear in love because perfect love casts out fear". Yes, God may reveal sin, but we have the knowledge that it is already forgiven; we do not need to hide in fear. We need to choose to let God heal what He can already see. That *is* being perfected in love. The more we are in God's presence, the more we are purified by our obedience to the truth; "Having purified your souls by your obedience to the truth for a sincere brotherly love, love one another earnestly from a pure heart" (1 Peter 1:22). Love only works from a pure heart and purified hearts come from obedience to the truth. God shines His light of truth through His presence right into our hearts. We obey when we let Him purify it, instead of pretending it isn't there. When things are shut up, just like inside a house, it starts to smell stale. We need freshness. It's time to open some windows and let in the light.

God knows our limited capacity. Jesus' presence with us can empower us to love beyond what we are capable. Just like light kills bacteria and mold, Jesus' presence naturally purifies us and our motives. Yet His presence does not incite guilt. It does not point out the wrong and leave us in the dark with it alone. He heals the wrong. Once healed, our capacity to love increases. Right now we can't love well, no matter how much abundance God can pour on, because we have these cracks in our cups. Until we give God complete access to heal and deal completely with every part of us, we can't be a vessel that loves well. Our capacity to hold God's love and let it spill over is handicapped.

This is hard to understand because when we see weakness and a lack of love in people, we judge them. When we see their inability to love spouse or children, we are inclined to pity them. I find, especially with women, that we are judging ourselves with this same strictness. We are disgusted with our own inability to love and we beat ourselves up to try harder and do more. Criticism is becoming the default language we speak to our hearts. When God sees our weakness and inability to love, He doesn't judge us, even though He justly can, He feels compassion on us and holds out what we need: Jesus. He stands there waiting to make us vessels that can share love with the world. We have to stop running from His presence.

Father, thank you that you are always enough. No matter what I may be lacking you are willing to provide it. Help me to be brave enough to invite your light to pierce my darkness and purify my love. I want to love well, of all the things I want, this is it! Help me be willing to do what it takes.

Teach me not to fear your presence in all the darkness of my soul but to throw wide the windows of my heart to let in the Light. Thank you that according to Philippians 2:13 you give me not only the desire but also the power to do what pleases you. I desperately need them both. Your turn

Everything I need for life and godliness, God is holding out to me. Through His precious promises and for His glory, I can love. I have to stop trying to do it my way, in my energy, and on my terms and embrace the provision God has supplied. It is going to mean that I have to "escape from the corruption that is in the world because of sinful desire", it wrecks love.

"Everything that goes into a life of pleasing God has been miraculously given to us by getting to know, personally and intimately, the One who invited us to God."

2 Peter 1:3 MSG

Personally and intimately getting to know God, that's how we are miraculously given everything needed to please God. His presence like light in the darkness heals and restores all that has been ruined.

Father, help me to love out of the abundance you offer daily and to stop trying to impress myself with myself. Help me to be able to admit that I am not enough and be strong enough to reach for you instead of buying into guilt and hiding from you. Teach me not to fear your presence. Show me your love; remind me that you are on my side and not against me to punish me. You have come that I might have life abundant. It is your nature to give. Make me into a vessel that can receive and overflow. Help me see you holding out your arms with everything I need for life and godliness. In Jesus name

Your turn

"Abiding in His love", "abide in my love", "abide in my love"....do you see the repetition? This phrase is used in this passage nine times. Nine times! You'd think God knew our propensity to miss the point. Look back at verse 11. Do you see the conclusion? If we abide in His love, His joy is in us and we are full. Full, as in lacking nothing. Isn't that what envy is, when we feel that we are lacking something. Envy is about abiding in myself, looking to myself and my own happiness. It produces no fruit. It steps right over what it has, to reach for what it doesn't because envy is never full.

Envy isn't just about wanting to possess things; it's about telling God that you don't have what you need to be full. It seeks to gain control over needs itself and shuts God out. Envy refuses what God is giving, which is all of Himself, for what we'd rather have. Quite simply, it's telling God that He isn't enough for us. When you break it down like that it sounds ludicrous that we would do that on a daily basis.

The word envy in Greek is phthonos (fthon'-os). It refers to the jealous envy that negatively "energizes" someone with an *embittered mind.* When we seek what we think we need before we seek God we are out of focus. We convince ourselves that we are responsible for our needs and making happiness happen. We aren't, and can't. This makes us incapable of seeing other people's needs because we can't look past ourselves and what we don't have. If our focus is constantly on what we are missing, then we don't ever see the abundance we have to give in love. 1 Thessalonians 3:12 says, "May the Lord make your love for one another grow and overflow". God made us to overflow on one another. We can't do that while constantly taking inventory of what's missing rather than seeing the things God has given.

In my own life, my struggle is often people. I often envy relationships that I don't possess. Satan knows that if he can convince me I am alone; he can get me distracted from focusing on all God wants for me to have. It is dangerous when we measure what we have by what we *perceive* others have been given. Our perceptions are skewed by our limited knowledge. God loves each of us fully. We are fully loved in the way we were created by Him to be loved. He is the only one with the knowledge to decide what we need. We must be careful to watch that we don't find our meaning or fullness in what we're blessed with, but the One who blesses.

Where are you constantly taking inventory of things that are missing rather than seeing the things God has given?

Father, thank you that you know and understand our needs. You, yourself are the solution. Help us better understand how to find our fullness in you alone. Help me to really look at my abundance and make a habit of thankfulness that displaces a bitter mind. Fill me Lord, that I may be truly full, lacking no good thing.

Your turn

Evening   Reread John 15:1–11

Listen to what God says to your heart. What are you seeking to fill yourself with?

Father, show me the things that I envy and show
me how a focus on the abundance you have given
and abiding in your presence can change the state
of my heart. Teach me thankfulness that makes
my heart whole (Psalm 9:1).
Your turn

Every time I read this passage it always disturbs me that envy is right in the same line as orgies. You would think I would get over the shock of it, but I guess I shouldn't. It should shock me that my sin of envy is right in a list of sins like sorcery, sexual immorality, and drunkenness. It should shock me into realizing that my sin is a big deal, big enough that Paul feels the need to specifically repeat conceit and envy in verse 26 without revisiting the ones that originally shocked me. Envy is just as pervasive as the rest of the list; it rots us from the inside. Unchecked, it leads to bitterness that can't help but spill out.

We've already talked about envy having to do with possessions. Often things we envy can be more than things, we can envy people's positions or their status. We can desire to be as loved or as popular as so and so. When I researched the Greek root of envy, something stuck out to me. The definition suggests an eagerness to possess not just things, but people. How do we possess people? Flattery can be a dangerous tool for the possession of people. It is a way to possess people's allegiance. How much do we seek people's allegiance? Do we say or do nice things for people because we love them or because it endears us to them? This is another area where we have to abide with God so that His light shines on our motives. The key to refining our motives is in verse 16 and repeated in verse 25. It's like the book ends of this passage. We have to walk by the Spirit so we do not gratify the flesh. Living by the Spirit is the solution to the whole list of sins in the middle! The closer our walk, the less our flesh trips us up.

Romans tells us to "Let love be genuine. Abhor what is evil; hold fast to what is good. Love one another with brotherly affection. Outdo one another in showing honor" (Romans 12:9&10). The Message translation phrases the beginning of verse 9 like this, "Love from the center of who you are; don't fake it". When we flatter, it is not genuine. It is twisting God's gift of encouragement into a tool for self-gain. We can love well when we have let God deal with our motives. He can judge them rightly and lead us to love genuinely with the gift of encouragement. It is a gift that is really needed today. If we are going to love from the center of who we are, then God has to be put in our center and self-removed.

God, you are the giver of friendship. You know that we need encouragement and genuine love. Help us not to seek people's flattery as a way to fill ourselves and let us in turn not use flattery to gain a false love. Give us a heart of wisdom that chooses words well. Help us be able to outdo each other in showing honor not as a competition but rather a furthering of the kingdom. Fill us with so much of yourself that we no longer feel the need to fill ourselves.

Your turn

Notice that in the closing verses David asks God to guard us from this generation forever. The way He does that is exposure to the Truth, Himself. We are exposed to this culture over and over and it can only be undone with exposure to God's refining presence.

Reflect back on verse 6, what is the refining tool God will use to keep us?

Father, thank you for the Truth that is your word. Thank you that as we exalt the Truth we are purified from our lies and double hearts. Search my heart and make me aware of lies that come from my lips and unite my heart to fear your name only (Psalm 86:11).
Your turn

As women, I am convinced we all feel we are never enough. I think we particularly feel this in relation to being wives and mothers. It may be the constant urgency in the role that seems to never end or the relentless world of comparison that face book and Pinterest have ushered in, but I don't believe we were meant to feel this way. When we do, we are buying into Satan's lie that we are still not enough. He's tricked us into accepting Jesus forgiveness of our sin, but still identifying ourselves with our sin. We know we are forgiven but we are forgetting about the power that comes with the cross and the Holy Spirit in our new identities. We need to see that we are not enough, and still believe that God knew that when He placed us in our specifically chosen role. He knew that our not enough is just where we need to be, empty so that He can fill. If we could grasp this and lean into our God who equips us with everything good for doing His will, and let Him work in us what is pleasing to Him, through Jesus Christ(Hebrews 13:21) … maybe we could take a breath. Breathe that truth in deeply! Jesus is enough; I can quit trying to be.

Love does not boast because it realizes that without Jesus it doesn't have a leg to stand on. Paul says in Galatians 6:14 that he would never boast in anything but the cross of Jesus Christ. He even says that this world and all of its interests were crucified to him. I wish that I could confidently say that all of the world's interests were crucified to me. What I can say is that God is working out my boasting issues and my desire for the world to think much of me. Praise Him that I can trust Him to finish the work.

We have to *know* and *believe* the love God has for us (1 John 4:6). Remember I said that verse has two parts. We need to know and believe how much God loves us, and that He has love for us, at our disposal to use on others. He has enough love to fill the caverness hole that echoes, "You are not enough!", and make us whole. Then, out of that abundance we can love others while forgetting ourselves because Jesus will be our enough.

Father, let us bring our fears of never being enough straight to you instead of trying to fill ourselves up with ourselves. Show us how to walk in step with the Spirit and be perfected in love so that we can love others as you have loved us. Your turn

We have been lavished in Love. We are children of God. That *is* our enough. The world does not need to recognize it; they didn't recognize Him. We can rest that the world's definition of "enough" doesn't apply to us, and doesn't nearly cover God's abundant enough.

God illustrated this point to me just the other day; He used my 2-year-old to do it. We were at our favorite greenhouse picking up some azaleas, and it had been raining for days. The puddles were legendary, but we were prepared having both worn our galoshes. Caleb picked the tiniest puddle to jump and splash in; he parked himself in it and continued having a wonderful time. It barely splashed. As a mother of boys I felt the need to help him get really dirty and proceeded to explain to him that this puddle didn't have enough mud. The words were no more than out of my mouth when I heard God clearly ask, "Enough for whom?" Caleb was fully engaged in the puddle in front of him and having a marvelous time, and I was taking it upon myself to redefine what should bring him joy. Why? Why do I listen when others try to redefine my joy? When the world tells me it isn't enough, why do I listen? Satan's game from the beginning was to try to get us to believe that God was not enough. I know it to be a lie, why do I listen?

What are some of the fears you have about not being enough?

Who are some of the people you fear you will not be enough for?

Take a minute to give those people back to Jesus. He is enough for them.

God thank you that when we run to You with our feelings of inadequacy, instead of telling us we are enough, you show us yourself. Help our inadequacies to usher us into your presence wanting more of you instead of trying to make ourselves seem adequate.

Your turn

"Living then, as every one of you does, in pure grace, it's important that you not misinterpret yourselves as people who are bringing this goodness to God. No, God brings it all to you. The only accurate way to understand ourselves is by what God is and by what he does for us." (Romans 12:3 MSG)

Ever misinterpret yourself? I do. Often the way that I misinterpret myself leads to misrepresentation of myself. I make myself look much better than I really am. (No, I am not just referring to make up, I will never ask you to stop wearing cover up). There is one specific place in our culture that immediately came to mind when I started thinking about misrepresentation: Facebook. Social media is an excellent place to boast, and it comes with the socially acceptable stamp of approval. It's a way of displaying the best of yourself while maintaining the approval of people you haven't had an actual conversation with in years. We don't need to just get the approval and admiration of the people closest to us, but their second cousins and grandmothers twice removed can also applaud how cool we really are. This is an excellent fix for the delicate ego.

Before you decide to hate me, I am not saying you can never get on Facebook again. I am saying it is wise to limit it and that in my life it has been good for me to take sabbaticals. If I don't, I am prone to boast and make myself look better than I am. Face book can be a dangerous tool of comparison for women too. It is often a misrepresentation or my misinterpretation of myself. It's okay if you have to read that twice. We can use social media to make us look like we have perfect children or perfect families, and no one does. I don't want to have been used by Satan to heighten another woman's insecurities because she has seen a misrepresentation of me. Love doesn't want others to feel less, so that it feels like more.

Social media isn't all bad. I have seen it genuinely used to boast about God. That is all we have to boast about. That is the only healthy comparison. When we see that the measuring stick is Jesus, we throw in the towel and realize that we don't need to compare; we just need Him. Instead of trying to convince God how cool we are and that He wants us on His team, we realize He *is* the team! I misinterpret myself by thinking I have any importance when I should get my only value in the fact that God, knowing that I offered Him nothing, loves me.

Father, help me with my interpretation of myself. Remind me that I am nothing without you. Also remind me that with You, I can be a force to be reckoned with because You are able to do immeasurably more than all I could ask or imagine according to your power at work within me (Ephesians 3:20). Let me be quick to boast of you and to identify unhealthy admiration of self. Your turn

How can you better love others when your misinterpretation of yourself is seen in light of Jesus?

Father, help me magnify and exalt you alone. Let me see myself clearly through your eyes and let that lead to a devotion to love others as I have been loved.

Your turn

Week 3

Love is not arrogant or rude

It does not insist on its own way.

Week 3 Intro
Love is not Arrogant or Rude
It does not insist on its own way

This week we have a triple hitter. We're dealing with sin left unchecked in us that leads to arrogant and rude behavior which leads to insisting on our own way and stepping on people. Like most sins I know, these are twisted from something God designed for good: the gift of knowledge.

Now don't get me wrong, knowledge is important, but it isn't one of the Big Three listed in 1 Corinthians 13. Those are only faith, hope, and love (v.13). Verse 8 assures us that knowledge won't last. When we finally see Jesus, all that we thought we knew will be blown away in the light of the glory of God. For now, we only see dimly as in a mirror (v.12). Arrogance has no place in God's presence. So likewise, God's presence is the key to dispelling arrogance. The key to dealing with arrogance is letting God's light shine on it and expose it.

Knowledge is still a gift. God created it with a great purpose. Romans 15 succinctly explains that, "Strength is for service not status. Each one of us needs to look after the good of the people around us" (verses 1&2 MSG). When knowledge is no longer looking after the good of the people around us, it oversteps its bounds and becomes arrogant or rude. We will either build people up or cause them to bleed out by how we choose to handle knowledge. It has to be tempered with God's presence and discernment. See God knows that we easily become too enamored with ourselves. He made us fragile so we could be reminded of our limits.

The third part of our triple hitter this week, insisting on our own way, makes me think of my children. Children are transformed from cute little balls of giggles and hugs into insane screaming lunatics when they don't get what they want. Parents can't wait for them to grow out of this phase. Sadly, I know lots of adults that never have; they just wrapped it up into better packaging. We call it manipulation.

Manipulation is a grown up and more socially acceptable tactic for insisting on your own way, but it completely eliminates thoughts of other people and focuses solely on how to get what it wants. I have been a manipulator; I've been really good at it. It's been one of my tactics to deal with fear. The illusion of control has at times given me a sense of safety, but it always leaves me unfulfilled because it's just an illusion. I am not in control, and when I try to pretend that I am, I am usurping God's rule over my life. The only time I am safe is when I am in the center of His will, not mine. As God deals gently with my heart over this issue, He assures me He is trustworthy, and I have seen that when I submit and pray rather than try to manipulate, He makes beautiful things that were never even in my plans.

This passage may seem out of place, but its principles can be applied to much more than food sacrificed to idols. "...Knowledge puffs up, but love builds up" (v.1). The word arrogance literally means puffed up. Knowledge is a powerful gift but when it puffs into arrogance we are in danger of destroying a brother for whom Christ died (v.11). Being right about something doesn't change people's actions, but loving them may. How many times have we been right at the expense of someone else's character or feelings?

These are examples of how arrogance has hurt love in my own life. I am sometimes arrogant with my children when I know that I am right and they are wrong. It is easy for me to play my parent card and tell them this is how it's going to be. But this isn't how God treats me. He is always right, but He doesn't silence me because He knows I am wrong. He lets me be heard, always. He never stops being right and He doesn't change the truth, but listening to me communicates His love for me. My children need this same assurance that they are loved. They need to be heard even when they are wrong. That is the kind of parenting God models for us. We can be right and not be arrogant. Children can have consequences and still feel loved. This truth transfers to all of our relationships not just our children.

I wonder how many fights and bitter feelings could have been avoided with my husband if I had listened more when I was *sure* I was right. I hate to think about how many times I have hurt a friend with too many words, imagining that I knew the answer. Plato knew the danger of too many words, "Wise men speak because they have something to say. Fools speak because they have to say something." I can't tell you how many times I wish I had been silent, but chose instead to fill the silence with my own arrogance.

Even in a situation where we are not wrong, how much more love is communicated through listening? We have to learn how to love in a world where people are not going to be perfect, including us. Love creates a safe place to be wrong, for me and others. Knowledge can be turned to wisdom when Love is added. It's the secret ingredient. The Love added needs to be Jesus; He adds the wisdom to our knowledge. Because He is a personal God, He has personal and individual answers to our circumstances. Only purposeful and ongoing contact with Him can help us know how and what to say, and He is very good at helping discern the when. It's been my experience that He is the only person who can shut me up, but I have to be in the habit of contact with His Spirit to discern His voice over mine.

> "Don't ever let being right talk you out of being kind." Bob Goff

Being right doesn't have to talk you out of being kind. The only way to be right and not be arrogant is to walk humbly with God. His presence, though comforting and encouraging, also keeps us in the light that exposes our own sin. Walking in close proximity to God works humility because that light allows us to see ourselves for what we really are: nothing without Christ.

What is one way that arrogance has inhibited love in your life?

Father, arrogance in our lives shows our need for you. We cannot love when we are arrogant because we can't see past our perceived goodness. The only goodness we have is Christ. He is the only thing in us of any worth. God give me patience with others when I am trying to lean on my own strength or knowledge. Help me see with your eyes. Hearts are won by love, arrogance only damages them.
Your turn

God protects us from our arrogance by making us fragile. We need often be reminded that we are clay and that God supplies all power to accomplish anything. One of God's great mercies to me has been letting me have chronic migraines. Yes, you read that correctly. It is a great mercy to me because it is a painful reminder of how much I need humility. In my heart of hearts, I used to think that migraines were a way of dramatizing headaches. I may have never said that out loud to anyone, but I thought it in my heart. It's embarrassing to even admit. Now that I suffer chronic migraines, not one goes by that I am not reminded of my arrogance.

Father, in your great mercy you remind each of us that we are only clay. Thank you for allowing our fragility as a tool for humility. When feeling proud of ourselves, let our reaction be reaching immediately for you. God give us ears that hear only what you think of us and drown out all other voices that we not become puffed up.
Your turn

There is a danger in knowledge when we forget where it comes from, and it can lead to being rude. When we presume that we have the answers, we step on others.

In my life, my tone of voice can come from arrogance. Tone is instrumental in the art of belittling. How I wish it wasn't an art form, but I know that it is. When we are rude to someone, we are communicating to them that we believe we are more important than them, or that they aren't worth our time. It belittles the person receiving our words and serves to make us feel above them.

Rudeness indicates a lack of respect. In truth, there are people that we need to love that we may not respect. It is hard to show love to someone you don't respect. It's one reason why loving people is so difficult. We have so much trouble not seeing the people for the sin. Often when we have trouble respecting someone, and sometimes that comes from a knowledge of their sin. This rudeness is tied so closely to arrogance because arrogance looks past our own sin but not theirs. We have no right to arrogance. We are not saved by our works of righteousness but according to His mercy (Titus 3:5). The problem lies not in the person we are having trouble respecting, but in our view of ourselves. The same mercy God applies to us is applied to them. We may see ourselves as farther along on the journey to sanctification, but any accomplishment in us is not to our credit, it is God who works in us.

We may not agree with a person or respect the decisions they are making, but speaking arrogantly or rudely will not persuade them of the truth. Jesus treated the sin and the person separately. He could hate the sin and still have love and compassion for the person. This never stopped Him from speaking truth into their life. He was not always received, but when He was, lives were changed and growth and maturity began. If we are rude and arrogant with the truth, it will not be heard, and love will not build up. Our knowledge of the truth can puff us up and give us an incorrect estimation of ourselves, or we can walk closely enough to God that that knowledge of the truth can shed light on us, keeping us humble enough to see others and compassionately share the truth with them. The key is in the closeness to God, abiding in Him and Him in us. He can give us discernment for what to say and when to stop. In my own life that last one is crucial. How often has arrogance lead me astray with too many words? How many times do I wish I had just stopped speaking one sentence sooner!!!!

God, just as the book of James warns us that no man can tame the tongue, remind us that you are not a man and you can tame our tongues. Let our tongues be used to glorify your name above ours and to spread the truth of the gospel.
Your turn

"Sin is not ended by multiplying words, but the prudent hold their tongues."

Proverbs 10:19 NIV

I like how the NIV indicates that words do not have power over sin. In holding our tongues, we often create space for the Holy Spirit to speak. Prayer is the best use of words.

Is there a time you can remember when your motives may have been pure, but your tongue ran on ahead of you?

Father, remind us that when words are many sin is not lacking. Teach us to measure the weight of our words before they are dropped. Let us feel your steady hand holding us back before we let emotions carry us places we never meant to go. Your turn

Arrogance isn't just limited to words we speak, but words we refuse to hear. We can allow arrogance to puff us up so that we become too large to see our own selves, kind of like being pregnant when you can no longer see your toes. When others point out sin in us, we can become defensive. I love verse 8, "But my eyes are toward you, O God, my Lord; in you I seek refuge; leave me not defenseless!". We don't need to defend ourselves; God did. Jesus is our defense. If our eyes are toward God, then we see how He loves us and we don't need to defend ourselves to man. With our eyes on God, we are safe to be wrong because we are loved.

I want you to note that verse 5 indicates that you accept rebukes and instruction from a righteous man. This does not include people's random opinions of you. It definitely does not include personal attacks or verbal abuse. Righteous men rebuke in love because they are being led by Love. If we are keeping our face toward God, it is easier to discern a righteous rebuke from a personal attack.

"Let a righteous man strike me – it is a kindness; let him rebuke me – it is oil for my head; let my head not refuse it."
                                                    Psalm 141:5a

Father, at the same time that we ask you to set a guard over our lips, we ask that you open our ears. Let us listen to the instruction and even rebuke of the righteous. Enable us to let go of pride that keeps us from hearing. Above all else, help us apply your word to ourselves. Let us be ready to receive any instruction that comes from its pages and be quick to obey.

Your turn

Did you note that in verse 10 and 13 it talks about fullness in Christ? Go back and read those two verses again. This whole passage is about unity in the body of Christ and love being the instrument that grows and builds it (v. 16). We aren't growing up in love, because we are stuck. We aren't dealing with our sins and it directly affects our fullness in Christ and capacity to love. I am ready to stop treading water. I want to be equipped to love. I want to deal with sin in my life so that I can love and build up the body and hasten the coming of Christ! I don't want to be a child tossed to and fro but rather attain unity of faith and the knowledge of the son of God, to mature manhood, to the measure of the stature of the *fullness* of Christ (v.13). He came to *fill* all things (v.10). He cannot fill a vessel that has not opened its lid to Him or that is incapable of holding the abundance. He needs vessels to fill that have been loved whole. We are meant to bear the fruit of love. We have become too busy with ourselves, nursing our hurts and coddling our sinfulness. We are broken and bruised and laden down with sins when the One who will take that burden and heal those wounds waits for us to let Him.

Arrogance and rudeness are the opposite of humility, gentleness, patience and bearing with one another in love (v. 2). If we are allowing ourselves to be arrogant we are no longer gentle and we see no reason to bear with a brother or sister. I want to be eager to maintain unity of the Spirit in the bond of peace (v.3). Let's renew our commitment to be purified and perfected in love.

Are there words that you have needed to hear, but don't want to accept?

Father, we want an eagerness to love. We ask that you work in us. Grow us up in every way. Show us how to speak the truth in love and build up the body of Christ in love. Show us ourselves and rather than shrink from what we see, help us place it in the light of your presence and be healed and cleansed of sin. Make us brave to confront sin in us. Thank you that your work of our forgiveness has already been accomplished.

Brian, my five-year-old, and I used to do this thing. It really came from this book about a Nut Brown Hare. The big hare and the little hare try to outdo each other in showing how much they love the other...very cute book. Anyway, back to Brian and me, our thing would start with me telling him I loved him. He would respond with the phrase, "I love you more than you love me". And then we would proceed to "play-argue" over who loved whom more. As innocent of a game as that was with my son, one day it struck a nerve in me. I realized that this is a game a lot of adults play. It's the "I'll love you if you love me" game. We sometimes even play the "I'll need you if you need me" game. This leaves us dangerously dependent on people for our identity and happiness. We can't let our love be reactionary. Then it isn't love, it's just emotion.

According to 1 Corinthians 13, love does not insist on its own way. There is so much packed into that little sentence. It makes me picture a fit being thrown by a child, screaming and hollering to get what they want. In actuality, adults have just learned to harness that emotion and turn it into manipulation to get what we want. Left to ourselves we find love useful, useful as a tool for manipulation. But love does not insist on its wants. We can love our friends so that they love us back the same way, and we can withhold that love when they don't return it the way we perceive that they should. We play this game back and forth, but we aren't trying to "outdo one another in honor" for the right reason. We try to outdo one another to incite guilt. And we use guilt as a way to pull people's emotions and get what we want.

Responding in love becomes harder when people demand our love. Children are crazy demanding of love...it's their nature, but adults demand our love when they haven't put away childish things (v.11). When we demand love it's because we aren't seeing clearly in that mirror Paul was talking about. The Perfect will come and when we really see Him we will understand that we are perfectly loved, and we will stop being so desperate for people's love. In the meantime, we have to fix our eyes on the truth and believe the love God has for us. We have to focus on the gift that "now we know in part" even if we don't know fully yet (v.12). God always gives enough. We have to focus on the enough He has given.

When people demand our love, it is a comfort to know that God does not demand our love. He does not love us to manipulate. God is free from us. When He does something for us, He does it out of choice. He is not swayed by compulsion, guilt, or manipulation. He died for us because He wanted to. We can rest in His love; because He doesn't have hidden motives. This freedom from us allows Him to love purely. It can free us to be able to love as well. We *can* rest in His love. It's one of the choices we get every day, scratch that every hour. It's backward that we should struggle to rest in His love, but the more we choose it, the easier it becomes.

Father, let me take what I know in part and let it help me rest in what I know will be revealed. Let hope produce faith in me. Free me from insisting on my own way. Free me from the use of manipulation with the ones I love. Show me your love that fills and keeps me from seeking to fill myself. Let me rest in Love.
Your turn

Additional journaling space

How are you being deceived into wanting your own way instead of accepting the good and perfect gifts already given you?

When we insist on our ideas and expectations of God, we don't limit Him but rather our own hearts. Our capacity to love the way we are intended depends heavily on our being fully loved. When we refuse God's gifts, we are actually refusing His love. Recognizing and receiving His love brings rest and peace into every day, every hour, every moment.

Father, give us eyes to recognize your good and perfect gifts in a world that distorts our vision. Release our grip on our own way, and keep those hands safely held in yours.

Your turn

I like things my way. I really do. I often marvel at the fact that my children do not always want to do things my way. In fact, we spend a lot of time on just this scenario. I love for things to be finished. I love the completion of projects like an entire house cleaned, a complete chapter or book read, a meal made to completion, you know things that I rarely enjoy with three children. As much as this can drive me crazy, I see more clearly how many times I must mirror my own children. God has such patience with me when again and again I don't want to do things His way. God's way almost always looks a lot differently than mine. Even when His way makes sense to me, it isn't often how I would choose to do it. For instance, this whole sanctification thing, pretty long and painful; it isn't what I would chose. If I could insist on my own way, I would have everything neat and perfect the day I became a Christian. But that isn't His way. His way is for me to struggle against my flesh day in and day out ... "producing in me endurance, and endurance producing character, and character producing hope, and hope does not put us to shame, because God's love has been poured into our hearts through the Holy Spirit who has been given to us" (Romans 5:3-5).

Insisting on my own way doesn't open up an avenue for me to have God's love poured into my heart. My sufferings and struggles open up my heart to God as an avenue to receive His love. I can insist on my own way, and miss all the love He wants to pour, or I can let go of all my desires to be perfect "now" and realize that the process is the relationship. And the relationship is everything.

This whole life is going to be about longing for what isn't finished. The small ways we do that, like when we desire completeness of our projects, just mirror what our hearts are really longing for. We long for heaven even when we don't know how to put it in those words. We long to be finished, to not struggle with flesh anymore and to see Jesus clearly. We long for perfection. We long to be transformed into His image. We have to let the longing keep us hopeful. Let it make us be brave to open our hearts for God to pour in love and produce endurance, character, and hope. We have to let go and do it His way because that is the only way it works. We should rejoice in the fact that God looks at all our undoneness, and instead of growing frustrated or impatient at our incompleteness, He bends to help us.

God help us recognize all our longings for what they really are, a desire for that Perfect that we lost in the fall. Thank you that you place that longing in our hearts to point to you. Let it draw us to you and not to our own ways of trying to fill it. Thank you that the culmination of this life, which seems long but is momentary in light of eternity, will be restoration and completion. Thank you that because of what Jesus has done, it is already finished. Release us from insistence on our way, and pour yourself into the spaces you create in our hearts.

Your turn

Additional journaling space

"We often view sin as evil action alone and miss the nature of sin itself. At its root, sin is simply grabbing for ourselves what God has not given us."

Wayne Jacobsen

How does this broaden your view of insisting on your own way?

Father, show us how your ways are higher than our ways and your thoughts ours. When we are puttering around here in our own darkness, help us to look up.

Your turn

Week 4
Love is not irritable or resentful.

Week 4 Intro
Resentment and Irritability

Resentment and Irritability are producers of bile in our hearts. They wreck love because they are hidden and spring up at unexpected times. They are the product of holes. Big chunks taken out of us by disappointments, hurts, failures, and crushing blows. These things open up holes in our hearts, and as we nurse these hurts our hearts fill with bile. Our love is then poisoned by it; it taints our reactions and responses. This is a result of not letting God really see and fully heal and restore us.

Healing is something that takes time. The world we live in has no patience for time. When we are sick, we want to be made better yesterday. In our rush to be better, we often end up remaining sick longer because we refuse to slow down and actually heal. We don't have the time. That's exactly what's wrong with our hearts; we won't take the time. We don't allow ourselves the rest and healing it takes to be made whole again. I don't want to take the time to heal the hurts because the process is painful and long. So instead, I choose to pretend it isn't there, and it waits in hidden places of my heart until something touches it, and then I react out of pain and bitterness that I have allowed to remain.

When this happens, I am so disappointed in myself that I start thinking that God is too. I become frustrated at my inability to heal myself. I deeply want God to be proud of me and my struggle leads me to think that He isn't. Satan has used this trick on me over and over. God gave me this picture that I want you to keep in your head as we go through this next week. As a parent, I am not more proud of my children when they have completely mastered the skill of riding a bike than I am when they fall for the fifteenth time and look to me for help again. I am just as proud in their attempts as their success. Their reaching for me in need of help is a precious thing. When my daughter cooks with me, I am not disappointed when she spills or gets egg shell in what we are making, I am enjoying my time with her, it's not just about the finished product. God feels the same about His children. The reaching for Him is our relationship. It means time spent with Him. He doesn't rush healing, and He is not more proud of us when we are healed than while we are in process. He is not proud of me because of my accomplishments anyhow. Isaiah assures us that the greatest of our successes are filthy rags. Anything accomplished through me was enabled by Him; I have no accomplishments outside of Christ. He is proud of me because He loves me.

Have you ever over reacted? Right, me neither. This would be a great place to insert the laughter/ crying emoji. In case you missed that sarcasm, let me just say that I over react all the time. You see over reactions are really just reactions. They only seem like the are too much because we can't see what is going on under the surface. Every action has a cause.

Enter irritability. You see, being irritable stems from irritation; it happens when something has gotten under your skin. Irritability is a reaction. It's a response to an action. The problem with irritability is that it is often a delayed response. It may be a reaction to something that happened quite some time ago. When a new little irritation occurs it can cause an over inflated reaction because of the old irritation left hiding just under the skin.

When I researched the Greek root for irritable in scripture I found the word *chole* meaning to be bilious or full of bile, enraged or angry. It is linked to the word choleric which is defined by Merriam Webster as, "easily moved to often unreasonable or excessive anger". All of this information went straight to one very personal example: colic. If you have ever had a colicky baby, you know where I am going with this. Colic is characterized by fits of crying that have no reasonable explanation. My children's colic was diagnosed as acid reflux. Literally bile rising up from the inside causing distress! We may not be able to see or name the distress in a colicky baby, but we know it's there. The same is true of irritable people. We may not know what is under the surface causing their reaction, but the anger is definitely there. The bile is rising up and causing them to lash out because of their pain.

We are incapable of love while nursing irritability. The Message translates the phrase "love is not irritable" as "doesn't fly off the handle". When we are with someone who is prone to outbursts of rage or flying off the handle, we do not feel safe. When we create anxiety in others because they do not know when we will respond with irritability, we cannot love them well.

We have to open our hearts to God rather than trying to push the bile back down. We have to own our hurt and anger with Him. What we read in James today shows us that this anger and irritability does not produce the righteousness of God. That is why we have to deal with it with God because once it's in there, it will come back up. When it does, it causes distress and pain for the person afflicted and those around them. This is more than an issue of self-control. It indicates something that needs dealt with so that it stops recurring, and we are set free from it. Different things may cause the bile to rise in us. It may be we are nursing selfishness, there are circumstances that we're having trouble dealing with, or we can be irritable at specific people (sometimes even justifiably angry at someone). God is the only one who can deal with these emotions. We have to give Him complete access to our hearts, knowing that what may hurt in the short term will take care of the bile in the long term.

Instead of reacting, we need to refocus. When we feel that bile start to rise, we need to ask God to help us recognize what is truly causing our irritability and then ask him to train us to refocus on Him and be filled with His love to heal us.

What are some things or people that you react to?

What may be the root cause?

God, help me chose to refocus instead of react.
Make my spirit sensitive to feel the bile start to
rise and make me quick to run to you for help
and healing. Thank You that you put divine
power at our disposal to destroy strongholds
(2Corinthians 10:4). With that in mind, help me
to bravely face myself. Thank you that I don't do
any of this alone.
Your turn

This morning I asked about some of the things or people we react irritably to. With that in mind answer the following question.

How can the implanted word save our souls in this situation? (If possible be specific)

Father, never let me be like the man who looks in a mirror and immediately forgets what he saw. Help me refocus my gaze on the perfect law, which is Jesus, and instead of turn away because of my sin, be drawn into His love. Deal with me according to your steadfast love.
Your turn

Irritability and defensiveness are often closely linked. We feel defensive when we are being attacked or have already been wounded. Irritability is bred by an attack that keeps coming or a wound that has been allowed to fester. This is still about our reaction where we should instead re-focus; it's a defensive reaction. We feel the need to defend ourselves from a real or perceived threat to our well-being.

Real threats are real because they have proven themselves. We have been wounded by them and are left raw. Rawness of soul creates irritability towards anyone who gets close to our wound. The wound itself can become a way of excusing our irritability. Embittered hearts are created this way. Bitterness seeps into the bones. There are many scientific studies that provide proof of bitterness and negativities effects on the physical body. This is another thing that we can't fix. The pain is real and all we can do on our own is react. We have to give God access to the depth of our pain. We have to be real when we have been wounded. Nowhere in scripture does God ask us to suck it up and be tough or pretend it didn't happen. He will acknowledge the damage, and He will repair it.

God has seen all of my affliction and the distress of my soul (v.7). He knows all the threats real or perceived. He has created a refuge from the plots of men and the strife of tongues and can hide us away in the cover of His presence (v.20). His presence will cover us. It's like the invisible shield that harsh comments and manipulating words can bounce right off. But the best thing about His presence is that it heals. While He is covering us in His presence and stands in our defense, His presence ministers to our wounded souls.

In reading any of the gospels we find Jesus healing people everywhere He went. Why do we think it is different with us? "And wherever he entered, into villages, or cities, or country, they laid the sick in the streets, and sought him that they might touch if it were but the border of his garment: and as many as touched him were made whole" Mark 6:56 (AKJV). We cannot be made whole if we don't allow Jesus near to touch.

Wounds that have taken a chunk out of us open up a big hole to either fill with bile or be filled with Christ, who heals. God allowing those wounds opens up more space for Himself to fill. It may involve time, but God can change our automatic reactions to pain. Instead of defending ourselves, we can take our pain to the One who is our defense.

Thank you that every wound I have ever received was not meant to leave me with a gaping hole, but was meant as access for you to make me whole. Let my heart take courage as I ask for your touch to heal.
Your turn

Evening   Read Romans 8:17&18
                                 (At least twice and out loud)

"Can anything ever separate us from Christ's love? Does it mean he no longer loves us if we have trouble or calamity, or are persecuted, or hungry, or destitute, or in danger, or threatened with death?" (Romans 8:35 NLT).

        Nothing can separate us from the love of Christ, except us. We can choose. We let our pain get between Christ and us when we act like it is bigger than Him. We can believe it to be greater than Him. We can also choose to let Him heal our pain by trusting Him. And by doing so, embrace His plans to make us whole and complete, lacking no good thing.

What pain has been nursed in you and turned to bitterness?

Father, thank you that even our pain is used to work out our salvation. It can be used to make beautiful things grow from us. Make us brave to face our pain and stop trying to treat our brokenness ourselves. We share in Jesus' pain when we choose to let you deal with our sin and embrace the pain of sanctification.
Your turn

Additional journaling space

Before God asked me to write this, I didn't realize how much of a problem I have with resentment. If I were to own one of these "un" characteristics of love, resentment is mine. I resent so many things. My love is hampered and poisoned by it. Resentment taints love - always. There are so many things people have done or haven't done that I have resented. The results of that resentment have always manifested in my actions because my actions can't help but come from the overflow of my heart (Luke 6:45).

I often try to "cover" others sins. I have a need for peace and for things to be unruffled. The problem is that I can't cover other people's sin. Only Jesus can do that; He alone can really bring peace. When I try to do it myself, I tell myself things like, "just forget it", or "try to love them", after all that's what Jesus would do. However, I have come to believe that it isn't what Jesus would do at all. He never, not once, pretended that sin didn't happen. Not once. I try to do that all the time! I specifically do this with my husband when he has hurt me or not lived up to an expectation. There are times that he has hurt me with thoughtless words, or acted selfishly, just like me. I have done those things. But if both of us just try to bury our hurt and pretend it didn't happen, no one gets closer to being perfected in love. We just sit in our own filth and stew. When I cover up someone's sin and try to pretend it didn't happen, no one is helped. The offending party isn't helped. They are enabled to sin again against me or someone else, and they are not gaining sanctifications work. Then there's me. I try to forget, and try to forgive, but when sin isn't acknowledged it lodges in places in our hearts. No matter how hard I try, unforgiveness breeds resentment.

Forgiveness is something that involves me and God. I cannot do it alone. It *can* happen without participation from the third party. The third, or injuring party can choose not to participate in restoration, and you can still forgive with God's work in you. But God is also about restoration of relationship. This is modeled in our standing before God. He has paid for our sin once for all. There is no sin of mine unforgiven, even future sins are already paid for. It is for my good that I need to confess sins to God, to restore relationship and to agree with God that I sinned so that it can be used to perfect me.

Don't get me wrong there are some cases in which I need to forgive and the sin can be acknowledged before God without the third party's involvement, and He can totally heal it in me. For example, if one of my children hurts me unknowingly, or if they cannot understand, it is totally appropriate to let God work things out and heal. There are situations where the offending party keeps offending over and over so there cannot be restoration. But there are also situations in which the loving thing to do is to tell the truth. It is always more loving for me to tell my husband how he has hurt me, and let him apologize and restore our hearts than it is for me to stuff it and let it seep out in little ways, like huffy tones or whispered comments. I don't know about you, but I am great at body language and tone to get my meaning across.

Making things okay and smoothing things over isn't my job. Trying to keep feathers unruffled isn't a spiritual gift. Sometimes feathers need ruffling for there to be real restoration. The problem with this truth is discerning when to obey by covering another's sin with forgiveness and letting God do the healing in your heart without involving the other person, and when to obey by loving the other person enough to do the hard thing and show them their sin so that they can be perfected in love.

The answer to this problem is in relationship. But I don't mean our relationship to the other person involved, I mean our relationship with God. This can only work when we are abiding with God so that He can show us the steps that He has already planned for us to take. It never works when done in raw emotion, and it doesn't ever involve hasty reactions.

"Therefore, confess your sins to one another and pray for one another,
that you may be healed.
The prayer of a righteous man has great power
as it is working."
Verse 16

God, heal us. Let us be brave enough to restore relationships broken by resentment, and at the same time let us only follow where you lead. Keep us. You alone are able to keep us blameless. Sift the resentment out of us with Love that we can see your love more clearly for what it is, our goodness. Change our automatic reactions and attitudes with one another and base them on truth, not on our emotions.
Your turn

Additional journaling space

Tonight I want you to really think about resentment in your life and where it comes from. Give God complete access to the areas of your heart that you don't even know exist. The truth is that there are people who have taken chunks of us, either so large or so repeatedly, that we have tried not to feel it anymore. Feel it, and let God deal with your emotions; our reactions are fueled by them. Let God handle them; He alone can fill.

What are some people or situations that you have come to resent?

Are there any people that you need to talk with?

Has your resentment wrecked even an aspect of a relationship that needs restoration?

God forgive my resentment and help me to let it go into your hands. Where people have wronged or hurt me, you were always present. If you allowed it, then the pain has a purpose. Help me to see that the purpose is bigger than the pain and then let go of my bitterness. Let me seek your presence and thank you for the promise that when I draw near to You, You draw near to me and I am healed. Then set not just me free of it, but also the people I have resented.

Your turn

Day 4   **Read 1 Thessalonians 5:23 & 24**

Resentment is trickily tied to guilt, now hear me well, I said guilt not conviction. God does not put guilt on us, we choose it for ourselves. Guilt is Satan's counterfeit of conviction. While conviction leads to repentance, guilt leads us to exalt our sin by focusing on it. It's a tricky way of exalting self. The more we focus on our self, the more we will feel shame and guilt. Since we are constantly reminding ourselves of our failure, we become resentful the moment we think someone else is reminding us of failure or implying failure in any way. I do this mostly with my spouse. Sometimes he will simply ask me a question and my state of mind leads me to interpret it as judgment. He won't have meant it that way at all. When my mental state is focused on my guilt, I am instantly defensive.

There are also times that I need to hear a little constructive criticism, but don't accept it because I perceive it as an attack. The answer is in perceiving my standing with Christ correctly and not letting Satan use guilt to make me react defensively. I need to recognize my guilty feelings and take them to God, because that is all they are...feelings. They are only emotions, not truth. When we stand in the truth of the gospel, we can filter criticism or perceived criticism through it and have the ability to respond rightly from the truth instead of our emotions. We can feel safe while being refined because we understand the love of the refiner. While we feel that He may love us less while refining us, the truth is He will never love us more than when He is faithfully perfecting us. His love is our only constant. That knowledge can help us willingly be perfected no matter what instruments are used for our perfection.

"The great thing to remember is that though our feelings come and go, His love for us does not. It is not wearied by our sin or indifference; and therefore, it is quite relentless in its determination that we shall be cured of those sins, at whatever cost to us, at whatever cost to Him." C.S. Lewis

We've become comfortable with what it cost Him, but don't want to be bothered with having to be uncomfortable to be made holy.

Father, help us not to resent loving correction from you in whatever form you bring it. Thank You that You keep us blameless and help us to recognize the voice of Satan when he comes to wield guilt. Let us be so grounded in love that when conviction comes, we can deal with it securely as we are assured of your constant love. You stand in my defense.
Your turn

He will sustain us guiltless to the end. God is faithful. He knows our weakness. He knows that dealing with sin would involve dealing with guilt and He made provision for it all. He is able to keep us blameless, without guilt. We have to believe Him and trust this truth over any emotion that seeks to overthrow it. Satan knows that guiltless children are dangerous. He wields this tool of his well. He knows that it paralyzes and hinders us from being refined and being purified to love because He understands what a powerful tool Love really is.

God let me recognize quickly when I am dealing with guilt so that I can bring those emotions to you. Keep me from elevating them in my mind until they become paralyzing, and I become resentful and defensive. Thank you for dying for my sin and setting me free from guilt.
Your turn

There is a specific time of day that reveals to me that I have not already obtained perfection. Bedtime is literally my nemesis. Some nights I am pretty sure Satan invented bedtime to destroy me. Even on a good day, it can totally undo me. I react irritably when my children want another drink or have to pee or even get scared and want to talk because I have idolized my rest time, my *me* time. My voice takes on annoyance at their intrusion. Then I feel guilt, and I resent that! Basically when I react out of the fear of losing the rest that I think I need, I am irritable, and then I sin in my reaction to others, which leads to guilt and then resentment because I just want a minute!!!! Is that too much to ask? Sound familiar?

God knows everything we need. He is willing to provide it, *but* we have to be content to let Him instead of trying to control things ourselves. We need to trust His love. (For real, I am repeating that to myself because I have not really learned it yet…I just know that it's true.) Sin started when Eve didn't trust God's love to provide what she needed and took things into her own hands. God and I have enough past together that I know when I step in faith and believe Him, He does not disappoint me. It may not meet the expectation I had in my mind, but it is always enough. He knows what we need, and it might not be what makes us comfortable. Rest and comfort are not the same. He agrees with our need for rest. He took rest himself.

I feel certain that getting rid of bedtime is not the answer to my problem. In fact, I am pretty sure that then I would have an issue with murder. So, what to do? It starts with me recognizing when I start to focus on myself. When I feel my blood start to boil because I feel my rights are being infringed on, I need to stop and refocus and see the rights that Jesus willingly gave up for me. He willingly offered himself out of love. He has "made me His own". In understanding and remembering His love for me, the rights I feel I need are overshadowed with the supply I already have. This is where the implanted word we talked about comes in! In James we saw that it was the answer to save our souls. Implanted doesn't mean I quickly look up a relevant verse. It means that I know that self is going to war with my soul, and I stock my arsenal ahead of time. Then I can fight back. I want to fight back! I want endurance to produce character and character to produce hope in me (Romans 5:3&4). I don't want my family to remember that I begrudgingly gave them my time. I want there to be love in all my moments with them. I want to serve them with the right heart. I want genuine love for them.

I will fail again, and I will battle with guilt. But I will stock truth in my arsenal and I won't go down easily. When I do, I will be quick to reach for God to pull me up. God doesn't expect perfection from us; He is perfection in us. He will work perfection through us and in us and to us until He is ready for us at home. We'll get tired, but Praise God He won't.

God, help me to recognize when I am focusing on myself and help me to remember Love. You have made me your own. Make me willing for you to work perfection in me while knowing that your motivation for doing so is love. Let this knowledge set me free and make me able to press on and hold true to what you have attained for me. Father, make me willing to be a vessel of love to the people who take the most from me because I know Your supply of Love does not run dry. Show me how to love them without resentment and irritability. Let my love help them see you more clearly.

Your turn

Satan's joy is to take the small parts of everyday and get them to add up to failure, failure to love and beat sin. Irritability is often a product of our failure to beat sin on our own; Satan wants us to give up what we have already attained (v.16). Satan gets us to focus on us!!! If he can get us too consumed with ourselves to look at God, we will continue to feel guilt at our failure. If Satan can get us to believe that we are stuck in guilt, then Love hasn't reached us and really healed us fully. If guilt is left to fester, irritability easily follows from the pain. God can pour an abundant amount of love into us for us to spill over, but we never fill when we are left with a cracked cup that leaks the abundance right out of the hole left by guilt. According to 1 Corinthians 1:8, Jesus will sustain us guiltless to the end. We need to recognize when we are giving up what He has already attained.

He doesn't expect perfection; He knows we are only dust. But we need to recognize that we are dust with the Holy Spirit of the Living God inside! When I am willing, He can use my dust.

Where have you expected perfection from yourself, and when you failed, guilt beat you until resentment and irritability took hold?

Father, look in my heart and root out the guilt that hides there. You are able to sustain me guiltless to the end. There is so much freedom in that! Root out the guilt in me to make room for

the abundance of your love to fill so that I can willingly spill over on others. Help me trust that you will never run out of love for me.
Your turn

Week 5

Love does not rejoice at wrongdoing but rejoices with the truth.
Love is patient and kind.

Week 5 Intro
Love does not rejoice at wrongdoing but rejoices with the truth.
Love is patient and kind.

Of all the traits we have gone through, I've got to say this one seemed easy. Who rejoices at wrongdoing? I mean no one sees the news and says, "WoooHooo! Yeah!". No one sees people being wronged and rejoices, right? Then I started to really think about this. As much as it pains me to admit, I can't say that I haven't ever taken a little comfort in others struggles. It has made me feel less alone, more normal. I'm still secretly hoping that I'm not the only person who struggles with the ugliness that can be in me. Embracing this truth about ourselves and rejoicing in Jesus revealing it to us, will bring us freedom from this ugliness.

This is how it works: the more time we spend with Jesus, the more light shines on us. He is light, in Him is no darkness, so when we spend time with that light, it searches out our dark places. Jesus sees our sin and refuses to leave us in it. That is something to rejoice in! That leaves us with a choice, will we rejoice with the revealed truth? It is crazy hard to rejoice with the truth of our revealed sin, but it's possible when we see it in light of how much He loves us. If we refuse to see it, that's when we are rejoicing in wrongdoing. When I refuse the truth, I am refusing a part of His love.

Not only do we have trouble rejoicing with the truth in our relationship with God, but this carries right over into our relationships with people. We have turned the idea of being patient and kind into something it was never intended to mean: "Be a doormat and never tell people the truth because it may affect their opinion of you", is found nowhere in the Bible. We as Christians are not called to lie about sin, ours or someone else's. I know this may shock you, so I will give you a moment to digest that. As we research the original language of the phrase "patient and kind" in this chapter of 1 Corinthians you will find that it isn't what you expected. It challenges us to learn how to really love people with the truth. The truth is freedom from pretense; pretending only hinders our ability to love in relationships. Notice I didn't say assault people with the truth. There is a distinct difference. Jesus set a perfect example of this in scripture. The way we learn it is to lean on Him for guidance.

The revealing truth, hearing it and telling it, demands action. If we are honest, we don't want to make the effort. It requires a lot of us. It requires a change in habits and a lot of time in prayer. But we need to grow up and realize that we are not called to easy. I'm determined that when and if I make it to being ancient, I mean really wrinkled, I will have earned every one of my wrinkles struggling for *real* life.

"And let us consider {thoughtfully} how we may encourage one another
to love and to do good deeds."
Hebrews 10:24 Amplified

Love does not rejoice at wrongdoing. It would be easy to say that this just means that we aren't to take pleasure in evil things like murder or sex trafficking. Labeling it this simply makes it easy for us to look right past it. However, it isn't that simple. I know that I have rejoiced at wrongdoing when I have been happy at someone else's failure. I think it's safe to say that we have all done this. It is especially easy to do when it applies to someone whom we perceive to have wronged us. We can delight in their failure as a way to make ourselves feel better or avenged in some way. Sadly enough, in my own heart it hasn't stopped there. I have secretly rejoiced over the failure of another who never hurt me. I simply rejoiced because it made them seem more human. It made me feel better about my own frail humanity. Neither one of these is something easy for me to admit. But in my heart it needs to be brought to light so that Jesus can deal with the root issue. I wouldn't need to make myself feel better if I were really functioning out of Jesus' love for me. I wouldn't be tempted to make myself seem better if I really understood that I am looked on with love ALL THE TIME. God sees me without blemish. I am the one whose vision is all skewed. God never loves me less. I have not attained perfection, but Jesus took my sin in His own body, all of it, and beat it once for all. I am free to draw near to God and He will draw near to me. There is nothing that stands between us unless I put it there. God does not compare me to any other Christian on the planet. All the comparing is summed up in the fact that none are worthy, not one. It would be like my children, after falling into the mud, to argue that one was cleaner than the other. I wouldn't let either of them into the living room covered in mud, no matter which one had a little less mud. They would both need a thorough cleaning with the hose.

The beauty of the verses we read is that they don't say anywhere that we just need to try harder. It says plainly, "the Lord make you increase and abound in love for one another…that *He* may establish your hearts blameless in holiness". Hard as it is for me to admit that my heart has been ugly enough to rejoice at wrongdoing, knowing that God doesn't love me any less makes me want to let Him bring the hose and clean off all the mud. Not because He wouldn't wrap His arms around me while I was covered head to toe, but because His love makes me want to overflow with love. The depravity of my own heart makes me see His heart more clearly.

Father, we pray that you enable us to really see Your love, the love that will pursue us until we are blameless and holy. You won't leave us in the mud, not because you're afraid we will bring mud into your house, but because you want us there to love. Let us invite your presence over and over into our days and minutes until your presence cleanses us and our motives and we are so filled with you that we KNOW Love and feel safety in it. Get to the root of the things that entangle us.

Your turn

"*Rejoice* in the Lord always; again I will say, *rejoice*"
Philippians 4:4

"*Rejoice* with those who *rejoice*…" Romans 12:15

"But *rejoice* insofar as you share Christ's sufferings, that you may also *rejoice* and be glad when his glory is revealed." 1 Peter 4:13

"But may the righteous be glad and *rejoice* before God…" Psalm 68:3 NIV

"Let us *rejoice* and be glad and give him glory!" Revelation 19:7 NIV

There are a whole slew of things we are to rejoice in, leave it to us to pick the one we aren't to rejoice in. What's funny about that is that when we rejoice in the correct things, it helps heal the very root of the problem that caused us to rejoice in wrongdoing.

Father, open our eyes to see more of you, and as we see, our souls can't help but rejoice. Teach us to be thankful because thankfulness breeds joy in us. It opens our eyes to the treasures we have in you. Help us see clearly so that we rejoice because of or in spite of our circumstances. Let us rejoice because there are no comparisons that matter. We are no longer found lacking. In Christ, we are abundantly supplied.

Your turn

Love rejoices with the truth. *The Message* translates this phrase as, "takes pleasure at the flowering of truth". I have this rose garden beside my porch, roses are one of my favorite things. In spring and summer you can immediately smell them when you go out my front door. It's beautiful! This verse makes me picture one of my roses as it opens up. I love roses because their flowering takes time; this allows an appreciation for the flower in all its stages of development. Truth is just like that. God doesn't rush us to all the truth at once. He has an appreciation for watching us unfold in all our stages of development. It is beautiful to Him to watch. He doesn't love the end product more. He brings everything we need to grow and His presence is just like the sun shining down.

Love can rejoice with the truth even when it is hard. Love can delight in a God who unfolds truth to us one petal at a time because He knows that is all we can take. If you are loved, you can rejoice. The unfolding of His word gives light and understanding. It discerns the heart (Hebrews 4:12). God's face shining on us is how we are perfected. Time spent sitting in God's presence is never wasted time; it's the absorption of His light that feeds our soul.

When God reveals the truth to us to help us grow, it is never harsh and abrupt. It is gentle, swiftly accurate, but gentle. Responding to the truth revealed is always our choice. God doesn't force us. Below is one of my favorite poems by Emily Dickinson. She had such a great way of painting pictures in the mind. It's my hope that she embraced the Truth about God and that He did indeed dazzle her.

"Tell all the Truth but tell it slant –
Success in circuit lies
Too bright for our infirm Delight
The Truth's superb surprise
As Lightning to the Children eased
With explanation kind
The truth must dazzle gradually
 or every man be blind –"

                              Emily Dickinson

        We are able to rejoice at the Truth because God never blinds us with it. He is gentle and He dazzle's gradually, knowing exactly what our hearts can hold. Real freedom and greater intimacy are found when we lay down our defenses and accept His love of us and His discipline of us.

How does letting the Truth search you enable you to love better?

Father, let us not ever fear or hide from the Light you shine in our hearts to make us grow. Thank you for dazzling gradually and knowing our limitations and providing for them. Help us to rejoice with the truth because we know it is only your love for us is Truth. Shine a new light on us and grow us.

Your turn

Evening   Romans 12:1&2

Try to read this again with fresh eyes. It's a familiar scripture.
Think about renewing your mind. Make sure you notice that
the verb is not a past tense, it hasn't happened once for all
time. God is in the business of making things new. The truth is
sometimes the abrasive scrub He uses to refinish a surface of
our heart that needs to be renewed. That can be hard to rejoice
in, but the finished product won't be.

**What is a truth that God is unfolding that you need to
realize that God will perfect in the process of His presence
over time?**

Father, help us not to run from the truth as
abrasive as it can be. Make us brave to renew our
minds daily and not to stagnate in the pleasures
of this world. Help us cling to you and embrace
the process instead of striving for the end.
Your turn

God's word is the way that truth is often revealed to us. Jesus prayed for His disciples to be sanctified in truth. He went a step farther and prayed for "those who will believe in me through their word" (v.20). That's us. We are those who believe in Him. So He prayed for us to be sanctified by the truth of God's word. The end of this sanctification was "that we would be one", "I in them, and you in me that they may become *perfectly* one so that the world may know that you sent me and loved them even as you loved me" (v.23 italics mine). The reason we have to be sanctified and made perfectly one is so that the world will know Love. Granted we will always be an imperfect picture of it, we need to strive to represent that love to a world that desperately wants a love that's real.

God designed us to want love and to desire relationship, with Him and with others. The truth is a big part of making that work. Walking in the truth brings freedom from pretense. If you don't acknowledge the truth about yourself, it can't help but affect your relationships. If you can't accept the truth about yourself, then if someone you love brings it to light, you will not accept it from them and the relationship is damaged.

Jesus asked that we would all be one, and one in Him. It is for Unity's sake that we have to accept the truth about ourselves and deal with it. We need to learn to rejoice in truth revealed about ourselves because it brings sanctification rather than try to deny or hide our faults. God can use lots of tools to bring to attention things that need to be dealt with in our hearts. Seriously, I believe He designed marriage and children to do just that. It is very hard to pretend with the people who live with you. So many times we struggle with the tools He uses instead of embracing the truth and struggling with our sin.

According to Romans 12:9, for love to be genuine we must abhor what is evil and cling to what is good. We have to turn from what is evil in us and cling to Jesus.

This kind of truth that brings sanctification and unity looks totally different from the world. We are *supposed* to look totally different from the world. If our relationships aren't different from the world, it is an indication of something missing.

How has pretense affected your relationships with others?

Father, help me to cling to the truth. Comfort me as you show me things that need dealt with in my life. Let me understand how you have loved me, and let my confidence in your love make me free to see and admit to others where I have sinned. I pray for unity that comes from oneness with you in my life and community.

Your turn

When we know and acknowledge the truth, it sets us free. Freedom from sin is found in the truth. Things brought into the Light aren't as scary or paralyzing as they seemed in the darkness.

Father, take off my blinders to myself. Show me the light of truth on my heart and help me to receive truth from others also. I pray for a community of friends that I can trust to urge me to oneness with the body and with you. Reveal to me the next step in my sanctification as only you can in love and let me receive it in love.

Your turn

Allow me here to rewind to the beginning of this study of 1 Corinthians 13 and talk about Love being patient and kind. I didn't forget it when we started, but intentionally placed it here because of how it relates to rejoicing with the truth.

The specific word for kindness in 1 Corinthians is the Greek word Chre`stos. It is defined as a useful kindness, serviceable and productive. "We have no adjective in English that conveys this blend of being *kind and good* at the same time" (M. Vincent). There is no word in our language that correctly conveys what was being expressed here. It is a kindness that does good to the receiver.

The word patient used in 1 Corinthians is from a blending of the Greek makro and thumos. Makro indicates long duration and thumos is an outburst of wrath, properly passionate driven behavior directed at sin. The blend of these is *makrothyméō* ("showing divinely-directed patience") is "longsuffering" because it only expresses anger *as the Lord directs* (i.e. is the opposite of being "quick-tempered").

If you are like me, these are not definitions that first come to mind when I think of the words kind and patient. Quite frankly upon reading them I didn't want to explore them. They seem weighty with responsibility. Not just to love those God has given us, but to love them for good. This specific kindness and patience blended together are unique. It makes me picture Paul speaking the truth for the hearers good. If Paul lived in this century, he would be anything but politically correct. Paul realized, in a way that we often don't, how short time is. The early church lived in expectation of

Jesus' return in a way we don't. They literally looked for Him to return every day. That made time short. If you had something that needed said, you best say it. Jesus did the same. He divinely understood the hearts of people. He knew what they wrestled with. As many people as flocked to Him, also turned from Him. They weren't willing to rejoice in the truth.

We need to learn to live with this same urgency because Jesus may come back at any moment. There are many times when we enable people to stay in their sin out of fear of what it might mean for us, or purely out of selfishness. We lack the courage to shrug off people's approval or judgment of us. We don't love people enough to show a kindness for their good. We only love as it serves our purposes, not in truth. Our interest in others often stops at where they can be useful to us, in meeting our needs.

Only God can truly see hearts. Only He can use broken people to help fix broken people. We aren't like Jesus, we have our own faults. But Jesus abides in us. The only time Jesus can use us to speak truth to others is when we are abiding in His presence. If you aren't abiding in Christ, then someone in love needs to come to you and ask you hard and important questions. If you are, there may be someone you need to ask hard and important questions about their walk. God loves us too much to let us waste time here. His kindness was not meant to lull us to sleep, but to lead us to repentance (Romans 2:4). We weren't put here to waste our time in idle talk. This isn't a waiting room where we are to distract ourselves with social media and unimportant things until our names are called. We are here to be perfected in love. We are here to build each other up in love until we attain unity and maturity and fullness in Christ.

Father, help us learn to take love seriously. We are to love as you have loved. Show us the responsibility we have for one another in love. Let our love abound with knowledge and discernment and let that work together to keep us pure and blameless (Philippians 1:9).

Your turn

*"So then let us pursue what makes for peace
and for mutual upbuilding."*

Peace is not an absence of conflict but rather a
reconciling of our hearts to God. The only way to love as
Christ loved us is to abide in Christ. God alone can discern a
heart, mine or others. The only way this kindness works for
good is if it is God directed. We are often too lazy to do the
seeking God first part, and that is why this has often failed.
We have to clothe ourselves with the presence of the Lord for
him to discern our motives and hearts. Only the presence of
the Lord can provide the discernment needed for kindness
that tells the truth. If you are thinking this sounds like a lot of
work, you are right. This requires a lot of prayer and time. It's
not for the weak at heart, but takes a lot of courage. Reality
here on earth is that there are people who will not receive
kindness and rejoice at the truth, they will turn from it and
quite possibly from you. The gospel is offensive because it
sheds light on what we cannot overcome: sin. It is the truth of
our powerlessness, but it opens a door to real power over sin
through the gift of Jesus. The power of the cross was not a
onetime power. It is available to beat sin in every life, every
day, all the time. Love overcomes sin, but it often goes unused
because we are too busy counting what it might cost.

*Father, make us courageous to pursue peace and
not to be a people who remain silent in fear. We,
as your church, need to mutually build each
other up as iron sharpens iron (Proverbs 27:17).
We need to embrace the sparks and be made better.*

Strengthen our hearts and our identities in you that we may hold our confidence to the end.
Your turn

We are meant to produce fruit; it's actually why we are still here. We can be "strengthened with all power, according to his glorious might for all endurance and patience with joy". These fruits are produced with His strength, not mine. Seriously, patience with joy has to clearly come from Him. The pairing of the words patience with joy is something yet to be seen in me. I may have patience on occasion, but I am not joyful about it.

According to Colossians 3:12, we are to put on "compassionate hearts, *kindness*, humility, meekness, and *patience*". These aren't things we can manufacture in ourselves. Rather, "as God's chosen ones holy and beloved", He gives them to us to put on. He gives us Himself to put on. Only He can do any of these things sincerely. We are instructed in Romans 13:14 to "clothe ourselves with the presence of the Lord Jesus Christ" (NLT). The best thing about this clothing we put on is that it is more than a disguise or a covering of what we really are. When we clothe ourselves with the presence of God we become who He says we are. His presence does more than cover us; it changes us. Colossians and Ephesians both instruct us to put on the new self created to be like God. But nowhere in scripture does it say try really hard to be like God. When we stop trying and put on the presence of God it happens naturally. The reason we don't do this is that to make room for the presence of God there's a lot of things we have to put off. It's our old self. When we understand how we are beloved of God it is easy to put off the old self and put on the new. It is seriously the best Spring cleaning you have ever given your closet. It's the one outfit that fits every situation! Now tell me that isn't fantastic.

So how do we do that practically? The way to clothe ourselves with God's presence is surrounding ourselves with God, in the morning, in the midst of our day, in what we listen to, as we lay down to sleep, etc. By what we listen to, I don't just mean your music. I mean what we choose to hear. There are voices struggling in our heads every day, we have to choose to listen to the ones that are truth and tune out the deception. Let the presence of God act as your filter. Let His word be your measure of truth. When the reality of His love is what we put on, it changes what comes out and goes in like a filter.

Father, give us a desire for your presence that is insatiable. Let us be so loved by you that the love of the world fades away. Help us to put on kindness and patience with joy. By clothing us with yourself change us, refine us, and perfect us. Filter all that goes in and all that comes out of us and let your perfect Love work in and through us. Your turn

How often do our words bring grace to those who hear them? What does it really mean to bring grace? How can my words bring grace to my family?

Now let me ask another question: How often do our words bring grace to our children? As parents, we are responsible to build our children up in love the same way God builds us. I fear in some ways that our desire for our children to understand grace has translated into a freedom from consequences. God allows us to feel consequences and uses exact words to describe our sinful state. He sees us clearly as we are and loves us. Our children need to understand that they are completely loved, but this does not mean a removal of consequences. There is a balance to be attained in parenting. I find that my speech brings much more grace when consequences have been given sooner. When my children are allowed to repeat a behavior, I become exasperated and take on a tone of anger inciting shame. It is more of a kindness to give them consequences than to look past their sin. God does not protect us from seeing our sinful nature and feeling it's debilitating awfulness. He allows it and uses it as a kindness to bring us to repentance. Repentance allows restoration and growth. Allowing consequences for our children does the exact same. Understand there is a difference between pointing out a child's sin and harping on it. One leads to repentance and the other to guilt. Leave room for the Holy Spirit to work conviction.

Father, let our words be full of grace and free of shame. Above all else let us communicate love without words. And let our speech bring grace to those that hear.
Your turn

Week 6
Love

Bears all things,
Believes all things,
Hopes all things,
Endures all things.

Week 6 Intro
Love
bears all things, believes all things, hopes all things,
endures all things, Love never ends.

Funny story, stick with me it is leading somewhere. So, I have always been a person who doesn't like medicine. I try to fix things the natural way. I have been like this since way before this whole new craze in natural medicine. I use oils and I have been known to put lavender on anything. It works; from burns to eczema and even cranky babies who don't want to sleep. I preach it! I put it on people who come in my home; they are usually willing participants. For my birthday this year I got a new iphone. Four days after receiving it, in an incident that involved a runaway very muddy dog, a rainstorm, and being late for one of my children's parties (I will leave that all to your imagination), it got wet. I mean it got really wet not put it in a bowl of rice wet. I called my long time best friend for some sympathy and as I boohooed about my phone she started to giggle. She asked me, through stifled laughter, "Did you put some lavender on it; I hear that works on everything". In case you are wondering, I do not recommend lavender on broken electronics, but everything else yes. The point of this little story is that though lavender works on lots of things, we have an even better natural healer at our disposal. There is nothing that Love doesn't treat; not a thing. It applies, and should be generously applied to every situation. Love is what beats sin, because Love is Jesus and there is no way to get enough of Him.

Jesus holds us up, that's how love can bear all things. It isn't on our shoulders; it's on His. We just have to reposition the weight where it belongs. He lightens our loads by His presence with us.

In Jesus we can believe all things, our belief in His words is our guard against Satan. Satan comes to distort the truth and deceive us. Love came that we may have life, full and abundant. It comes to us in direct proportion to our belief. Check out any of the gospels.

Jesus makes it possible for us to hope all things. He is our hope, "we who have fled for refuge might have strong encouragement to hold fast to the hope set before us. We have this as a sure and steadfast anchor of the soul, a hope that enters into the inner place behind the curtain where Jesus has gone as a forerunner on our behalf" (Hebrews 6:18b-20a). This hope we have in Jesus can make us able to love people who will fail us, because He never will.

Only Jesus makes it possible for us to endure. We can endure the imperfection of life on this planet because one day we will see the perfect face to face and, "we will be like him for we shall see him as he is" (1John 3:2). We endure because of our future. We know the end game. We are only here a little while and He is coming back for us. We have to bridge the gap between knowing that this isn't our home and living like this isn't our home.

Love is Jesus and Jesus came so that we could overcome the world. Love is the secret super power waiting to be unleashed on a world full of hurt. It's the only thing that heals life on this earth, and it's who is coming back for us. We have to hold that truth in front of us always. We are on our last week of study. It's my prayer that we won't stop here because it's so easy to say we are finished when we aren't. We have to weave these truths and scriptures into our daily lives and let them color our individual situations. I can't give you parameters for your individual situations but the Holy Spirit can. We have to lean in heavy to scripture directed by the Spirit and listen to what He says for every day, *every* day.

The word bear used here is the Greek "stego" meaning cover, conceal or bear with. This properly means to place under roof, or cover over, to endure because shielded. When clothed in the presence of the Lord, we can bear all things because His covering is holding the weight. It's like if we are the house, and He is the roof. Nothing can "fall" on us before passing through Him first. He takes the weight out of it; he takes the impact. We are able to bear all things because we let Him bear it. He is perfectly willing and able to do this for us, and He has shown it again and again. "He himself bore our sins in his body on the tree, that we might die to sin and live to righteousness. By His wounds we are healed" (1 Peter 2:24). The testament of the cross is that Jesus bore our sins, all of them for all time, and if He can bear that, I am certain there is nothing else He will not bear for us. The second part of the verse is just as important. He died for us willingly without any deal for our surrender to Him. But He did die that we *might* die to sin and live to righteousness. We have the opportunity to die to sin and be set free from ,it and we can live to righteousness. It's a choice. We aren't *made* righteous. It's just offered. Please do not misunderstand, our righteousness is all a work of God, but we must surrender to be made righteous by Him. Jesus' pain was sin itself. He braved the pain of letting God deal with all sin in His own body. We share in His sufferings when we let God deal with sin in our bodies and embrace that pain for the sake of sanctification. 2 Corinthians 4:10 says that we are, "always carrying in the body the death of Jesus so that the life of Jesus may be manifested in our bodies". Carrying the death of Jesus in our bodies means that we are letting Jesus work the death of sin in us that we may manifest real life: Jesus. For Him to be seen, we have to die. We bear that every day that we chose to let Him work the death of sin in us.

Galatians 6:17 says, "From now on let no one cause me trouble, for I bear on my body the marks of Jesus". I want to bear on my body the marks of Jesus. Bearing the marks of Jesus on my body is bearing the marks of love. I may never bear scars on my back from being beaten because of my love for Jesus, but I can be willingly poured out as a drink offering. I can bear in my body the marks of motherhood, or the marks of singlehood, the marks of the brokenhearted, the marks of sickness, or the marks of loss. Whatever and wherever He has called me; He will bear with me. I can bear the marks of pain and suffering in whatever form they come because I know that He bears them with me, and they serve a purpose. There is nothing I will bear alone, ever. Every mark I bear will serve to set me free to live in righteousness.

What are some burdens that you need to let God take the weight of?

How can thankfulness for His willingly bearing the burden of sin for us take the weight of our burdens?

Father, help me to willingly bear the marks of Jesus on my body. Give me joy in the fact that not only did Jesus die for me, but He lives to make me holy as He is Holy. Help us to "put to death the deeds of the body" by the Spirit. Though perfection will not be attained in this life; He is our guarantee of an eternity with the Perfect. Keep our eyes fixed on eternity that our feet may plot a path of purpose for all our days here.

Your turn

We can love and bear with one another because He bears with us. When we put on love, we put on the presence of God. Inviting God's presence is a protection over us. It covers and bears our load. Bearing with one another can mean forgiving one another as we have been forgiven. That means with no strings attached. It can mean having compassion on another or just incredible patience. If we are willingly bearing one another's burdens, it can only be because Christ is bearing ours. Otherwise, even the broadest of shoulders could not carry the burdens of another with our own. If we were to wait until we are no longer struggling with sin to help another, then no one would ever be able to help.

Paul wrote these words to the brothers in Philippi, "Even if I am to be poured out as a drink offering upon the sacrificial offering of your faith, I am glad and rejoice with you all" (Philippians 2:17).

How does being able to be joyfully poured out relate to being made full in Christ?

How does forgiveness alleviate another's burden?

Father, make me willing to be poured out as a drink offering for those whom you have allowed me to love. Show and teach me how it can be a joy. Teach me how bearing with one another in love leads to being bound together in perfect harmony. Show me how to guard my heart in the giving so that I don't resent what is being taken because I can see clearly what I am being given. Your turn

What we believe controls us. This is as much a scientific as a spiritual proof. My children can prove it to me any day of the week. I can prove it to myself easily by my actions on any given day. When I feel pressure to perform, I can be controlled by time. When I believe that I am in control of my own life, I can be completely controlled by anxiety. When I feel something may be taken from me, I can be completely controlled by fear. Whatever it is that we are believing, it will control all of our actions.

What we believe is pivotal to who we become. Sin entered this world because Eve did not really believe that God loved her, she believed He was holding out on her. For the love of Christ to control us, we have to believe in His love. When we believe in His love for us, we trust Him, and only then are we willingly controlled by Love. This is the work that God asks of us, and it came straight from Jesus own mouth in John 6:29, "Jesus replied, 'this is the work [service] that God asks of you: that you believe in the One whom He has sent [that you cleave to, trust, rely on, and have faith in His messenger]'" (AMP). It seems easy enough when you say that what God really wants from us is for us to believe Him, but working out that belief in our daily lives is not that simple. I love the amplified version of this verse so much because of the phrase "cleave to". Some days I've just got to hang on with all I have. It's so easy to believe fear and anxiety over the love of Christ. They seem more tangible and masquerade as actions that accomplish something, when in reality they accomplish nothing. Believing in the love of God changes everything. Need tangible examples? Check out the New Testament. Everything those believers accomplished was because of their belief in God. It's why we are called "Believers"!

We do not easily believe people we have no knowledge of. The knowledge we have of Jesus is what solidifies our belief in Him "for the love of Christ controls us, because we have concluded this: that one has died for all, therefore all have died;" (2 Corinthians 5:14). I love how the NIV translates "control" as "compel" in this verse. We are not controlled as a robot; we are compelled to love because of Love. The word compelled carries with it the idea of being unable to help yourself. We are to be compelled to love others by the overwhelming belief that God loves us.

How do we train ourselves to believe the love of God?

Father, let us be compelled by Love. Let our belief in your love for us completely take us over so that we cannot help ourselves and love spills out from the joy of being full of your love. Teach us how to cleave to and rely on your love and keep us from believing the other voices that clamor for our focus.
Your turn

"We ought always to give thanks to God for you, brothers,
as is right because your faith is growing abundantly, and the love of every one of you for one another is increasing."
2 Thessalonians 1:3

This verse says it all: their faith was growing abundantly and consequently so was their love for one another. When our faith in God increases, the abundance of His love fills our cups so that we can't help but overflow.

God, we ask in your faithfulness that you grant us power to believe all that you are. Let our belief grow until it is all we can see in front of us, let that belief shape how we see others. Let our love for one another increase because it can't help but grow with the abundance.
Your turn

I love that the ESV renders this verse with, "the steadfastness of hope in our Lord Jesus Christ", where others use the word, "endurance". I love the word steadfastness. It's unmoving. We have steadfastness of hope because our hope is placed in *The* steadfast. I feel like the conclusion of the verse is the reason for the beginning. Because of the work of faith in me, I can labor in love which produces a steadfast hope of heaven. The work of faith in us allows us to have a hope in all things. All things, from God's hand, can accomplish our sanctification, so we are free to experience hope in all things. Faith, Hope, and Love are the catalysts that make us fit for heaven. That is why these are the three that endure (1 Corinthians 13:13). We can hope all things because we know Love. We know Jesus.

Father, let the work of faith in me produce a labor of love that increases my hope of heaven. Thank you that here is not my final destination. Thank you for the promise that you have gone to prepare a place for me. Let that knowledge allow me to be set free of the binding idea that I must make a place for myself.
Your turn

Evening   Read Romans 5:5 (NAS)
                                  Below

"And hope does not disappoint because the love of
God has been poured out within our hearts
through the Holy Spirit who was given to us."

      Love enables hope. We can hope all things because exposure to Love (Jesus) takes away all our jadedness. Every disappointment we have fades in comparison to the one who will not disappoint. The love of God has been poured out within our hearts through the Holy Spirit!

      What disappointments or shattered expectations do you need to bring to God that His love can pour into your heart and heal your hope?

"In the morning, O Lord, you hear my voice; in
the morning I lay my requests before you and wait
in expectation."

                          Psalm 5:3

How often do we pray with this expectation? Do we expect that God will not disappoint, or do we pray half-heartedly?

Father, we ask that you heal where our hearts have been broken. Enable our hope by covering our disappointments with your love that never disappoints. Pour out your love into our healed hearts that hope can spring forth genuinely and be an avenue of love. Your turn

Endure is the Greek word hupomeno (hoop-om-en-o). It really sounds like a character in a Dr. Seuss book. I picture it as a purple elephant like character with big floppy ears. It *actually* means to remain behind, to await, stand my ground, persevere. We endure with confidence. That's what Hebrews said. It promises that if we don't throw away our confidence there is a great reward.

Have you ever felt left behind? It's a terrible lonely feeling. You aren't sure which way to go or how to feel or where to begin. We, as followers of Jesus, have been left behind, but there is a distinct difference that changes our futures. We are here to await a return. We aren't left behind by someone who has moved on; we were left by someone who is returning soon. This totally changes our course of action. The one returning for us is coming back because He loves us. We aren't at a loss not knowing which way to go. We are here to prepare for a return and to persuade as many people as we can to come Jesus loves them too.

Endurance is a waiting game. Soo what do we do with the time? We can either resign ourselves to the here and now and live life the way most of the world does in distraction, or we can wait with purpose and expectation *every* day. The book of Acts chapter 1 verses 10&11 holds my favorite account of the Ascension of Jesus. After Jesus disappears in the clouds the disciples all stayed gazing up at the clouds until two men appeared in white robes and said:

What are you doing? Why are we just staring at the sky here guys? Clearly that is a paraphrase. It's the attitude I imagine the angels had, but this speaks to me so many times. I get my head in the clouds and forget that my feet are still on earth for a purpose. James 1:4 instructs us to "let it grow, for when your endurance is fully developed, you will be perfect and complete, needing nothing" (NLT). We have need of endurance. We need to grow; it's the purpose for which we're still here. We are too complacent in our sin. Here we are remaining behind, treading water! We are not here to wait while staring up at the clouds. When Jesus gets here, we'll know it! In the meantime, we are here to become fully grown producing fruit in Love.

In Mathew, Jesus says that... "the love of many will grow cold, but the one who endures to the end will be saved" (24:12&13). When we get distracted with the world, we let our love grow cold. While we wait, we must kindle our love that we remember our purpose. That is the way to endure. Abiding in God as He abides in us and letting Him perfect us in love is the only way to move forward while we wait. It reminds us why we're here, who we're waiting for, and why.

What are some ways to kindle our love from growing cold?

How will this help us endure to the end?

God, we have desperate need for endurance. In a world where we wait for nothing, we need discipline to persevere. But we know that all of our best efforts will fail. Only Love can produce this work in us. Woo us with your love, the kind that makes our feet want to dance and get moving. Get our heads out of the clouds while we are still here! Remind us of our purpose and let that fill us to abundance with you. Let it be so intoxicating that our cares become light and momentary in light of eternity.

Your turn

"God desires all people to be saved
and to come to the knowledge of the truth."

"The Lord is not slow in fulfilling his promise as
some count slowness, but is patient toward you,
not wishing that any should perish, but that all
should reach repentance."

We are still here because of Love. It's the reason we aren't taken directly to heaven after salvation. Not because of our love, but because of God's crazy love. It is not God's will that even one should perish. We remain here so that we can shine as a light to a dark world. I want to shine well and hasten Jesus' coming.

God, help us to focus on the eternal over the temporal even in the little decisions that we make. Help us live to love as if you are coming for us tomorrow! Oh that you would! Yet I love you all the more because I know that you wait out of love. Your turn

We don't get a list of ten things to do anymore, according to Jesus, we just get the one, Love the Lord your God with all your heart, all your soul, and all your mind, and love your neighbor as yourself (Matthew 22:37). Jesus knows that if we really understand love and loving Him, we can't help but love others. It will just flow. Abiding in God is our one action for love. It's all summed up in that. We abide with God because we love Him and as we abide our love for Him grows. As we are in His presence, we are changed by it. He heals all that needs healed in us, and shows us where we need set free of sin. As we are perfected, we are able to better love because we have been loved. Love will flow out of full cups that have been cleansed and made holy for honorable use (2 Timothy 2:21). When done right, it isn't even work. God has promised that His burden is light. I am beginning just now to really understand that. And this is just the beginning. We have only uncovered the truth, now God is going to use that truth to do wonderful things in our lives.

"Let all that you do be done in love" (2 Corinthians 16:13b). Now we work out how this takes shape in our lives. We invite Jesus into all that we do, and then it will get done in love. Let me be clear, we won't get *our* agendas done in love, but this will work to get *His* agenda done in love. He will decide what we do and what we say no to. If we listen to Him, we can say no without guilt, and we can correspondingly say yes with joy because we know it's what He chose and He will provide. So now that you think this study is over, it's just really beginning. Now, it's on you to abide with God. That's it, final instructions and parting words. No lists, no ten step plan, just that one step. We are blessed to live in a time where we are under the new law, and that law is written on our hearts (Hebrews 8:10). We have access to as much God as we want. It is a blessed gift; let's take advantage of it.

The best part of this to me is the multiplication of obedient's blessing. Our children will see love at work in us, and they will learn that obedience comes from love not fear. Their obedience will bless others and so on. God works beauty from our obedience every time. He multiplies it's blessing through generations. Our family resemblance keeps growing.

God, help us to simply keep our eyes on you. Let us see the unseen. Pour your love into our hearts through the Holy Spirit (Hebrews 5:5) and let it produce a crazy hope in us. As you become more and more real to us as we practice your presence let Love flow from your heart through ours to overcome sin.
Your turn

Evening

> "May the Lord direct your hearts
> to the love of God
> and the steadfastness of Christ."
> 2 Thessalonians 3:5

Ladies, this is my parting prayer for you, that the Lord direct your hearts to His love. It has been a blessing to have been with you through this study. I will borrow these words from Paul, to write the same things to you is no trouble to me and is safe for you. Abide in His love.

Close with your prayer to God committing to abide in His love every day and be filled to overflowing with it.

Notes

Week 1 Day 2 evening - Evening   Wayne Jacobsen, *How He Loves Me.* Copyright 2007 by Wayne Jacobson. Windblown Media.

Week 3 Day 1 - Plato quotation, www.goodreads.com

Week 3 Day 5 - Evening   Wayne Jacobsen, *How He Loves Me.* Copyright 2007 by Wayne Jacobson. Windblown Media.

Week 4 Day 4 - C.S. Lewis, *Mere Christianity.* New York: Harper Collins, 1980.

Week 5 Day 2 - Emily Dickinson, "Tell all the Truth but tell it slant" from *the Poems of Emily Dickinson*: Reading Edition, ed by Ralph w Franklin. Copyright 1998 by Emily Dickinson. Reprinted by permission of The Belknap Press of Harvard University Press.

All Hebrew of Greek word studies were from biblehub.com

About the Author

Lauren Mitchell is an author and teacher who spends most of her time chasing her three children and the rest of it chasing the heart of God. She has a passion for prayer and sharing her own struggles to help others learn God's steadfast love. She desires for her life, writing, and speaking to make others yearn for a closer walk with God.

Photo by: ejamescarderphotography.com

You can visit Lauren anytime at
www.laurenmitchellwrites.com

Or @laurenmitchellwrites

Other books by Lauren Mitchell

Steadfast: A Study of the Prayer that Made David's Whole Heart Rely on a Steadfast God

Things Pondered from a Mother's Heart

Available on Amazon or wherever fine books are sold

Things Pondered From a Mother's Heart

Lauren Mitchell

Acknowledgements

The first person to always thank is my husband. He loves me so well. He is always supportive of this dream God has given me and he holds the fort down so well when I am gone speaking or teaching. He will never know what His support of all of this has meant to my heart and how it has spoken his love for me without words.

Lorey, you are my Barnabus. Thank you for many nights of reading manuscripts out loud to check for my laurenisms that you know, but others may not understand. You will always be my favorite editor. I will never forget your reading part of this book really loud in Starbucks so that everyone could hear it because they needed it.

Sabrina, Denise, and Fawn you have supported me in the spiritual realms and prayed tirelessly for me. I love you, ladies.

To all my favorites who never miss a book signing or speaking engagement if it's in the Tri-State area and have done this study with me multiple times. You are in my heart forever.

Made in the USA
Lexington, KY
15 November 2019